PHYSICAL SCIENCE DAYBOOK

In Collaboration with NSTA

GREAT S**O**URCE·
EDUCATION GROUP
A Houghton Mifflin Company

Acknowledgments

Reviewers

Alberta M. Hix
Oakland Mills Middle School
Columbia, Maryland

Douglas Rummel
St. Mark's School of Texas
Dallas, Texas

Charles Harmon
Los Angeles Unified School District
Los Angeles, California

Credits

Writing: Bill Smith Studio
Editorial: Great Source: Sarah Martin, Kathy Kellman, Marianne Knowles, Susan Rogalski; Bill Smith Studio
Design: Great Source: Richard Spencer; Bill Smith Studio
Production Management: Great Source: Evelyn Curley; Bill Smith Studio
Cover Design: Bill Smith Studio

National Science Teachers Association: Tyson Brown, Carol Duval, Juliana Texley, Patricia Warren, Charlene Czerniak

Photos

Page 4a: PhotoDisc; **4b:** Jeff Tinsley, courtesy of the Smithsonian Institution; **5a:** Photographic Image Objects; **5b:** PhotoDisc; **6a:** PhotoDisc; **6b:** PhotoDisc; **7:** PhotoDisc; **8:** PhotoDisc; **9:** Image State; **11:** Corel; **12–13:** Corel; **14:** Corel; **16–17:** ArtToday; **18a:** Corel; **18b:** PhotoDisc; **20:** PhotoDisc; **21:** Image 100; **22–23:** Corbis Royalty Free; **24–25:** ArtToday; **27:** © Leonard de Selva/CORBIS; **30:** ArtToday; **32–33:** Corel; **34:** Corel; **37a:** ArtToday; **37b:** Corel; **37c:** Corel; **38–39:** Corel; **40:** Phillip Greenspun courtesy of James McLurkin; **41:** Jeff Tinsley, courtesy of the Smithsonian Institution; **42:** Photographic Image Objects; **43:** Corel; **44–45:** Corbis Royalty Free; **46:** Joel Page, Associated Press, AP; **47:** courtesy of Segway LLC; **48:** courtesy of Segway LLC; **48:** Eyewire; **48–49:** ArtToday; **50:** Digital Vision; **51:** Library Of Congress; **52:** ©Tony Anderson/Getty Images; **53:** PhotoDisc; **54:** PhotoDisc; **55:** Photodisc; **56:** © Kelly Overton **57:** © Kelly Overton; **58–59:** PhotoDisc; **60:** © Patrice Ceisel/Visuals Unlimited; **62:** © Bettmannn/CORBIS; **66:** Library of Congress; **68:** ArtToday; **70–71:** PhotoDisc; **72:** © Wayne R. Bilenduke/ Getty Images; **74:** © E. Haucke, G. Ochocki Productions/Photo Researchers; **79:** © Hashimoto Noboru/CORBIS Sygma; **80–81:** PhotoDisc; **83:** Photographic Image Objects; **84:** © Farnsworth Archive; **84–85:** PhotoDisc; **86:** PhotoDisc; **88:** Hulto Archive; **89:** © Bettmann/CORBIS; **90–91:** ArtToday; **92:** Photos.com; **93:** PhotoDisc; **94:** Corel; **94–95:** Corel: **96–97:** PhotoDisc; **99:** NASA; **102–103:** Corel; **104:** PhotoDisc; **106–107:** ArtToday; **107:** © Christie Silver; **108:** Artville; **109:** PhotoDisc; **110–111:** DigitalVision; **112:** PhotoDisc; **114:** ArtToday; **116:** Corbis Royalty Free; **117:** Corel; **120:** Patricia Lanza/California Science Center; **121:** PhotoSpin; **122–123:** PhotoDisc; **124:** © Pool/Reuters/TimePix; **126–127:** Corel; **128:** PhotoDisc; **130:** PhotoDisc; **132–133:** Corel; **133:** PhotoDisc; **134:** Corel; **135:** PhotoDisc; **136:** ArtToday; **136–137:** PhotoDisc; **138:** Corel; **139:** Corel; **141:** Hulton Archive/Getty Images; **142:** PhotoDisc; **144–145:** ArtToday; **146a:** Nicholas Bergkessel/Photo Researchers, Inc. **146b:** PhotoDisc; **148–149:** ArtToday; **150:** © Charles D. Winters/Photo Researchers, Inc. **151:** PhotoDisc; **152–153:** PhotoDisc; **154–155:** Corel; **155a:** Corel; **155b:** Corel; **155c:** Corel; **155d:** Corel; **156:** © Christoph Hellhake/Getty Images; **158:** Jonelle Weaver/FoodPix; **159:** © Swim Ink/CORBIS; **160–161:** PhotoDisc; **162:** Corel; **164–165:** PhotoDisc; **168:** Kenneth Ingham; **171:** © Jim Pisarowicz; **171:** PhotoDisc; **173:** © Bettmann/CORBIS; **174:** ArtToday; **176:** Digital Vision; **177:** Corel; **178:** PhotoDisc; **179:** © Owen Franken/CORBIS; **180–181:** PhotoSpin; **182:** © Kathryn Kleinman/Food Pix; **183:** © Ron Leighton; **186:** Getty Images; **188:** PhotoDisc; **189:** PhotoDisc; **190–191:** PhotoDisc; **192:** Corel; **194:** Corel; **194–195:** Corbis; **196:** Corel; **196–197:** Corel; **197:** PhotoDisc; **198:** © Biophoto Associates/Photo Researchers Inc. **200:** © AP Photo/Elise Amendola; **204:** Jose Torres; **204–205:** Corel; **206–207:** Photos.com; **208:** Michael Branscom/Lemelson –MIT program; **209:** © Eric Long/ Smithsonian Institution; **212:** © Ron Leighton; **213:** © Ron Leighton; **214–215:** ArtToday; **216:** Artville

Cover: Image Farm

Illustration: All illustrations by Thomas Gagliano, except page 54, Kenneth Batelman and page 82, Jeff Thompson.

_sci_LINKS® is a registered trademark of the National Science Teachers Association. The _sci_LINKS® service includes copyrighted materials and is owned and provided by the National Science Teachers Association. All Rights Reserved.

Printed in the United States of America.
International Standard Book Number: 0–669-49249-3
5 6 7 8 9 10 — DBH — 10 09 08 07 06 05

Sources

10 From "Thrown for a Loop...Roller Coaster Science," by Samatha Beres. Copyright © 1999 by Scientific American, Inc. All rights reserved.

14 Louis Bloomfield, howthingswork.virginia.edu, 2002.

20 © Exploratorium, www.exploratorium.edu

24 Glubock, Shirley and Alfred Tamarin. *Olympic Games in Ancient Greece.* © HarperCollins, 1976.

28 Hickam, Homer H., Jr. *Rocket Boys.* New York: Delacorte, 1998. (pages 295–296).

30, 36 Boston Museum of Science, Inventor's Workshop. (http://www.mos.org/sln/Leonardo/Inventor'sWorkshop.html)

40 "MIT Senior's Robot Begets 'Ant' Farm." MIT Tech Talk. *MIT News.* Massachusetts Institute of Technology. (http://web.mit.edu/newsoffice/nr/1995/40009.html)

42 From "With the Right Equipment, Cows Can Be Trained to Milk Themselves" by Diane Langipan. Popular Science Newsfiles. (www.popsci.com) Popular Science 2002.

46 Used with permission from *TIME for Kids* magazine, © 2002

52 "Can a Static Charge on Plastic Playground Equipment Harm Someone?" *ScienceNet QuickLinks.* (www.sciencenet.org.uk)

52 Fowler, Steve. "Are Children's Slides at Fast Food Restaurants a Static Hazard?" *ESD Journal.* Fowler Associates, Inc. (www.esdjournal.com)

56 Reprinted with permission of *The Associated Press.*

60 Frostick, Robert. *An Amazon Adventure—Electric Eel.* (http://jajhs.kana.k12.wv.us/amazon/eel.htm)

62, 66, 68 From "AMERICAN EXPERIENCE" at www.pbs.org/wgbh/amex/Copyright © 2002 WGBH/Boston.

72 From *Aurora: The Mysterious Northern Lights.* Copyright © 1994 by Candace Savage. Published by Douglas & McIntyre Ltd. Reprinted by permission of the publisher.

74 Wollard, Kathy. "Sea Turtles' Magnetic Personalities." *Newsday.* 6 August 2002.

78 Adapted from "Fast Track" by Chana Stiefel, published in SCHOLASTIC SCIENCE WORLD, March 23, 1998. Copyright © 1998 by Scholastic Inc. All rights reserved. Used by permission of Scholastic Inc.

82 Excerpt from "Philo T. Farnsworth: Plowboy Inventor" from *Brainstorm! The Stories of Twenty American Kid Inventors* by Tom Tucker. Copyright © 1996 by Tom Tucker. Reprinted by permission of Farrar, Straus and Giroux, LLC.

86 Sandburg, Carl. *Chicago Poems.* 1916.

88 From *Mathematicians Are People, Too. Stories from the Lives of Great Mathematicians, Vol. 2* by Luetta Reimer and Wilbert Reimer. © 1995 by Pearson Education, Inc., publishing as Dale Seymour Publications. Used by permission.

94 Excerpt from *The Voyage of the Frog* by Gary Paulsen. Published by Orchard Books, an imprint of Scholastic Inc. Copyright © 1989 by Gary Paulsen. Reprinted with permission.

98 Plait, Phil. "What Does Outer Space Feel Like?" Online posting. *Phil Plait's Bad Astronomy: Mad Science.* (http://www.badastronomy.com). © Phil Plait. All Rights Reserved.

102 Special permission granted, *Current Health magazine*, published and copyrighted by Weekly Reader Corporation. All rights reserved.

104 This excerpt from an article by Denise Brehm appeared in *MIT Tech Talk.* It is reprinted with permission of the Massachusetts Institute of Technology, where Professor Walter Lewin teaches physics.

108 From "The Physics of Music," by Jake Miller. Copyright © 1998 by Scientific American, Inc. All rights reserved.

112 Reproduced with permission from www.NewScientist.com

116 Hardy, Mat. "Science: Color Scheme." *Beyond 2000.* (http://www.beyond2000.com).

120 *California Science Center Web site: Magic, the Science of Illusion.* "Living Head Backstage." (http://www.magicexhibit.org)

124 "The Balloon that Flew around the World." *Scientific American Explorer.* November 1999.

128 "Why is an Apple Pie's Sauce Always Hotter Than the Pastry Even Though They Have Been Cooked on the Same Heat?" Rob Landolfi, *Physlink.com Expert, Physics & Astronomy Online:* (http://www.physlink.com)

130 "Polartec: Building a Better Sheep" by Jonathan Dorn, *Backpacker*, April 1998.

138 Gallant, Roy. *Explorers of the Atom.* Doubleday and Co., 1974.

142 HOW COME?/ DISCOVERIES FOR YOUNG PEOPLE/ Countless Particles Make a Flake, NEWSDAY (Long Island, NY); May 15, 2001, p. C2 (Copyright © 2001 Kathy Wollard)

146 What's Outdoors, by Doug Collicutt, *Winnipeg Free Press, Sunday Magazine*: Feb. 4, 2001. (http://www.naturenorth.com/column/col18.html).

152 Meisenheimer, Karen. "Experts from UF Dig Up World's Longest Solidified Lightning Bolt." *UF News.* University of Florida. (http://www.napa.ufl.edu)

158 From "The Tale of Henri Nestlé and Daniel Peter." *Chocolate Valley.com.* Indotronix International Corporation (www.chocolatevalley.com)

162 Wolke, Robert. *What Einstein Didn't Know.*

166 HOW COME?/Atoms Like To Stick Together, Newsday (Long Island, N.Y.) Oct. 21, 1997, p. C2. Copyright © 1997, Kathy Wollard.

168 Eliot, John L. "Deadly Haven." National Geographic Magazine. (http://www.nationalgeographic.com)

172 "Montshire Minute: Carbon." Montshire Museum of Science. (http://www.montshire.net/minute/mm011126.html)

178 "Better Hair Through Chemistry: It's Enough to Curl Your Hair." The Exploratorium. (www.exploratorium.edu)

182 "What Exactly is Jell-O Made from? How Does it work?" *How Stuff Works.* (http://www.howstuffworks.com)

186 From POPCORN DAYS AND BUTTERMILK NIGHTS by Gary Paulsen, copyright © 1983 by Gary Paulsen. Used by permission of Lodestar Books, an affiliate of Dutton Children's Books, an imprint of Penguin Putnam Books for Young Readers, a division of Penguin Putnam, Inc. All rights reserved.

188 "Irving Prager's Chocolate Dump Cake." *Carnegie Mellon: School of Computer Science.* Carnegie Mellon University. (http://www.cs.cmu.edu)

192 The Virtues of Venom. (http://chainreaction.asu.edu/desert/digin/venom.htm) © Diane Boudreau

196 From THE HISTORIES by Herodotus, translated by Aubrey de Sélincourt, revised by John Marincola (Penguin Classics 1954, Second revised edition 1996) Translation copyright 1954 by Aubrey de Sélincourt. Revised edition copyright © John Marincola, 1996.

198 Darwin, Charles. *The Voyage of the Beagle.*

200 Harris, Tom. "How Light Sticks Work." *How Stuff Works.* (http://www.howstuffworks.com/light-stick.html)

204 Torres, Dr. Jose. "Diving Under Antarctic Ice!" The University of South Florida: College of Marine Sciences. (http://www.marine.usf.edu)

208 "Innovative Lives." Jerome and Dorothy Lemelson Center. National Museum of American History, Behring Center. © 2002 Smithsonian Institution.

212 "MIT Inventor of the Week: Nathaniel Wyeth." Massachusetts Institute of Technology. (http://web.mit.edu/invent/www/inventorsR-Z/wyeth.html)

216 From "What Exactly is the Physical or Chemical Process That Makes Adhesive Tape Sticky?" Copyright © 1997 by Scientific American, Inc. All rights reserved.

UNIT 3 Sound, Light, and Heat — 92

UNIT 5   Interactions of Matter — 176

Motion and Forces

Balls bounce, apples fall, wheels roll, and birds fly. Forces in nature produce many different types of motion. Sir Isaac Newton was the first person to describe the physical laws that explain how objects around us move. Over the centuries, engineers have used their understanding of motion and forces to build many tools and machines that are useful to us— and some that are just plain fun.

In this unit you'll build a track to determine the relationship between the two forms of energy that keep a roller coaster zipping up and down. Newton's laws of motion will help you explain the movement of a rocket. You'll examine some simple machines, and learn about some modern machines that show off the most recent technology.

Did You Know?

Engineers in Seattle have developed a robot that washes windows. The toaster-sized robot has been used to clean a giant glass pyramid that sits outside the Louvre museum in Paris, France. Suction cups hold the robot to the pyramid as it moves around. A big squeegee and rotating brush mounted on the robot's hood do the cleaning. The whole thing is controlled by a joystick.

THE CHAPTERS IN THIS UNIT ARE . . .

CHAPTER 1:

Up, Down, and All Around

Find Out: What kind of roller coaster track gives you the fastest ride?

CHAPTER 2:

May the Force Be With You

Find Out: What can Sir Isaac Newton teach you about skateboarding tricks?

CHAPTER 3:

Da Vinci's Designs

Find Out: How did an artist use his knowledge of forces to invent new machines?

CHAPTER 4:

Modern Machines

Find Out: How are robots used on a dairy farm?

Up, Down, and All Around

The Wild Ride

How does a roller coaster ride pull you this way and that? Hop on and see.

You bought your ticket. You waited in line. Now it's time for the wild ride. Suddenly—whoosh!—you're falling and turning and mashing into the side of the roller coaster car as it whips around corners!

Roller coaster rides are a thrill. English physicist Sir Isaac Newton (1642–1727) never rode on a roller coaster, but he did describe the forces acting on objects moving up and down and all around.

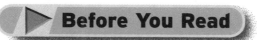 **▶ Before You Read**

THINK ABOUT IT Imagine that you are riding in a car or bus. The table lists ways a car might move. Fill in the table to describe how your body would move (or feel) with each movement of the car.

What the car does	How my body moves or feels
Starts moving	
Speeds up	
Slows down	
Makes a right turn	
Makes a left turn	
Comes to a stop	

▶ Read

Here's what happens when a moving car changes direction.

A Law of Motion

Why do I feel glued to the [out]side [edge] of the roller coaster car when it whips around a curve?

Think about what happens if you make a sudden turn when you're driving in a car. If you turn left, you seem to feel a mysterious force pushing you to the right: the kids in the back seat wind up pressed against the passenger-side door. Why is that? Well, before you started your turn, both the car and your body were moving in a straight line. And as Isaac Newton noticed hundreds of years ago, objects move in a straight line unless a force acts to change their motion. (This is part of what we now call Newton's first law of motion.) So when the car begins to turn left, your body keeps going straight for a while—until the car door gets in your way. The same is true on a roller coaster: you keep going straight until the roller coaster car pushes you to the side.

From: Beres, Samantha. "Roller Coaster Science."
Scientific American Explorations.

Underline the statement that describes part of Newton's first law of motion.

Newton's first law says that objects tend to resist a change in motion. Circle any sentences in the reading that describe an object resisting a change in motion.

FIND OUT MORE

SCIENCESAURUS

SCILINKS.
THE WORLD'S A CLICK AWAY

www.scilinks.org
Keyword: Inertia
Code: GSPD01

11

PICTURE THIS Sir Isaac Newton discovered that an object at rest tends to stay at rest. Newton also found that an object in motion tends to keep moving at the same speed and in the same direction. So, things tend to keep on doing what they are doing—unless something else happens to them. That something else is called an unbalanced force.

The diagram below shows the top view (looking down from above) of a roller coaster car. Each picture is a snapshot of the car in a different position as it moves along the track. Look at the position of the rider (X) in the first picture. Imagine that the rider can slide across the seat. Draw the position of the rider at the other two points on the track. Add arrows to show the direction the *rider* (not the car) is moving at each point.

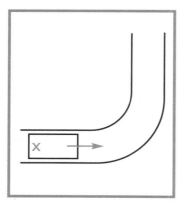 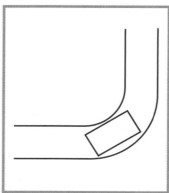 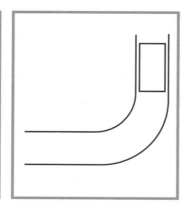

▶ *In what direction is the roller coaster rider moving in the first picture?*

_____

▶ *What was the unbalanced force that changed the rider's direction of motion?*

_____

_____

▶ *After the turn, in what direction do the rider and car continue to move? Explain your answer in terms of Newton's first law.*

_____

_____

_____

_____

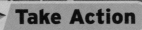 **Take Action**

PLAY BALL Imagine that you are a reporter for a science magazine sent to cover a baseball game. You watch as the pitcher throws a ball to the batter, who clobbers the ball with his bat, sending it sailing into the air for a home run.

▶ *Draw a three-part diagram showing the ball's position and direction of motion at three stages: as the ball is moving toward the batter; as the batter strikes the ball; as the ball sails into the air. Also identify and label the unbalanced force that acted on the ball to change its direction of motion.*

▶ *Below your diagrams, describe the pitch and the hit for your magazine story. Try to make the story exciting while still explaining the science of what happens to the ball.*

Up, Down, and All Around

To the Top!

You've got potential—energy, that is.

The chains creak as the roller coaster you are riding is dragged up the first hill. You reach the top. *This isn't so bad*, you think to yourself. The car hesitates for a second. Then it plunges downhill, picking up speed. The thrill you feel has a lot to do with energy changing forms. It's exciting, and it's physics!

 **Before You Read**

COMPARING ENERGY FORMS Imagine climbing the ladder of a high dive. When you get to the platform, you walk to the far edge and pause. At that moment, standing high above the water, you have potential energy. *Potential energy* is the energy an object has because of its position or its height. The higher the diving platform, the more potential energy you have. Now imagine diving off the platform. As you dive, your potential energy is converted to *kinetic energy*—the energy of motion.

Think of other examples of when people or objects have potential energy that changes to kinetic energy. Fill in the chart with your ideas. Some examples are already filled in to get you started.

Object or Person	Position with Potential Energy	Motion Showing Kinetic Energy
Rubber band	Stretched out	Snapping back
Ball	In the air after it was tossed	Falling back

UNIT 1: MOTION AND FORCES

> **Read**

Here's how Dr. Louis Bloomfield, a physics professor, explains potential and kinetic energy on a roller coaster.

HOW DOES A ROLLER COASTER WORK?

A roller coaster is [basically] a gravity-powered train. When the chain pulls the train up the first hill, it transfers an enormous amount of energy to that train. This energy initially takes the form of gravitational potential energy—energy stored in the gravitational force between the train and the earth. But once the train begins to descend the first hill, that gravitational potential energy becomes kinetic energy—the energy of motion. The roller coaster reaches maximum speed at the bottom of the first hill, when all of its gravitational potential energy has been converted to kinetic energy. It then rushes up the second hill, slowing down and converting some of its kinetic energy back into gravitational potential energy. This conversion of energy back and forth between the two forms continues. [B]ut energy is gradually lost to friction and air resistance, so that the ride becomes less and less intense until finally it comes to a stop.

transfer: to move from one place to another
initially: at first
descend: move downward
maximum: most, greatest
converted: changed
conversion: change

friction: the force that resists motion, causing objects to slow down and stop
air resistance: friction caused as an object moves through air
intense: strong

From: Bloomfield, Louis A. "How Does a Roller Coaster Work?" (www.howthingswork.virginia.edu)

Underline the first time potential energy is changed to kinetic energy.

Circle the first time kinetic energy is changed to potential energy (not including when the chain pulls the train up the hill to begin the ride).

FIND OUT MORE

SCIENCESAURUS
Forms of Energy   300

SCILINKS
THE WORLD'S A CLICK AWAY

www.scilinks.org
Keyword: Kinetic/ Potential Energy
Code: GSPD02

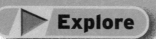

SEQUENCE THE ENERGY CHANGES Professor Bloomfield explains that an object has gravitational potential energy because of its height above the ground. Gravity is the force of attraction that exists between all pairs of objects. The greater the mass of the objects, the greater the force of attraction is. Since Earth is so massive compared to other objects nearby, we are usually only aware of the gravitational force due to Earth's mass. As the chain pulls the roller coaster car up the hill, farther and farther away from Earth, the car gains more and more gravitational potential energy.

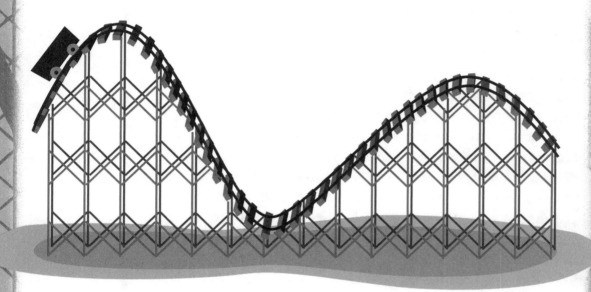

▶ *At which point on the track will the car's gravitational potential energy be the greatest? Label this point "GPE."*

▶ *At which point on the track will the car's kinetic energy be the greatest? Label this point "KE."*

▶ *Use a small triangle (△) to label three places where an energy conversion is taking place.*

MAKE AN INFERENCE Consider where on a hill a roller coaster car moves the slowest, and where on a hill it moves the fastest. How does the car's kinetic energy seem to be related to its speed?

_____

_____

_____

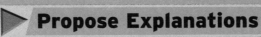
APPLY THE CONCEPT Imagine once again that you are on the platform of a high dive. On the diagram below, draw and label your position in the following three places:

1. *gravitational potential energy greatest, kinetic energy least*
2. *gravitational potential energy and kinetic energy about equal*
3. *gravitational potential energy least, kinetic energy greatest*

▶ *Describe the energy change that takes place as you dive off the platform.*

_____

_____

_____

_____

Up, Down, and All Around

The Big Drop

Have you got what it takes to go the distance?

Higher, faster, farther! The higher a roller coaster car, the more potential (stored) energy it has. The more potential energy it has, the more kinetic (motion) energy it will have when it reaches the bottom of the hill. But will the car have enough kinetic energy to roll up that next hill?

 Experiment

GOING THE DISTANCE

Test your own ideas about roller coaster track design.

What You Need:

- one marble
- pipe insulation sliced lengthwise (2-3 meters)
- masking tape
- two chairs
- measuring tape
- pencil
- stopwatch

What to Do:

1. Set up the track in a semicircular shape as shown.
2. Hold the marble at the top of one side of the track. Measure its height from the floor and record it in the table. This is starting point A.
3. Let the marble go. Measure how many seconds the marble rolls before it comes to a complete stop. Record the time in the table.
4. Repeat two more times and find the average roll time. Record the average in the table.
5. Now mark any lower spot on the track to start the marble from. This is starting point B. Measure the height from the floor and record it in the table. Repeat steps 3 and 4.
6. Study your results for starting points A and B. How do you think the starting height affects the total time the marble rolls? Choose a third starting point to test your hypothesis. Write a prediction about the results using an "if/then" statement: IF something happens, THEN something else will happen.

_____

_____

7. Measure the starting height and record it. Repeat steps 3 and 4, starting the marble at the new position.

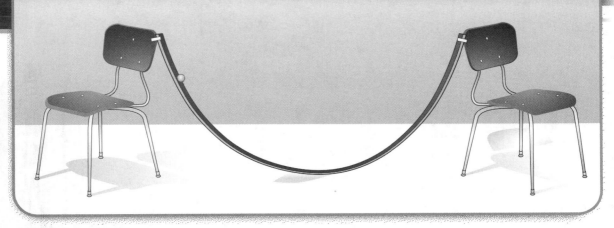

What Do You See?

Starting Point	Height (cm)	Roll Time #1 (s)	Roll Time #2 (s)	Roll Time #3 (s)	Average Roll Time (s)
A (top of track)					
B (lower spot)					
C (your choice)					

▶ Propose Explanations

DRAW CONCLUSIONS

▶ *Look at your prediction from step 6. How does your data support or not support your hypothesis?*

_____

_____

MAKE INFERENCES Kinetic energy is the energy an object has because of its motion.

▶ *Which starting point height gave the marble the most kinetic energy? What evidence do you have to support your answer?*

_____

_____

Potential energy is the energy an object has because of its position. The marble's potential energy is converted to kinetic energy as it rolls down the track.

▶ *What can you infer about which starting position provided the greatest amount of potential energy?*

_____

_____

FIND OUT MORE

SCIENCESAURUS

Testing
  Hypotheses   007
Gathering Data   009
Recording Data   010
Drawing
  Conclusions   013
Forms of Energy 300

SCILINKS.
THE WORLD'S A CLICK AWAY

www.scilinks.org
Keyword: Kinetic/
  Potential Energy
Code: GSPD02

May the Force Be With You

On Board With Forces

Can understanding physics improve your skateboard tricks?

Skateboarders love to perform, but like all performers they need lots of practice with basics. A stunt called the *ollie*, jumping up in the air with the board under their feet, is one of those basics. The physics is basic, too. A skateboarder just creates an unbalanced force on the board to make it pop up and follow his feet into the air.

 Before You Read

HOW DO THOSE TRICKS WORK? Skateboard stunts can seem like magic until you understand the science that makes them possible. Think of a trick you do, perhaps on skates, on a trampoline, in a pool, or another place. Describe in detail the actions needed to make the trick work. Use words like *push, crouch, twist, crunch, slam,* or *lean.*

_____

_____

_____

_____

_____

_____

_____

_____

_____

_____

▶ Read

In skateboarding lingo, an *ollie* is a jump. The jump is usually done while rolling forward, but the physics is the same whether the skateboard is moving fast, slow, or not at all. The jump begins when the skater bends his knees and jumps. Here's what happens next.

FORCES IN THE OLLIE

[As the skater jumps upward,] his rear foot exerts a much greater force on the tail of the board than his front foot does on the nose, causing the [tail to drop.] As the tail strikes the ground, the ground exerts a large upward force on the tail. The result of this upward force is that the board bounces up....

With the board now completely in the air, the skater slides his front foot forward [and] ...begins to push his front foot down, ...leveling out the board. Meanwhile, he lifts his rear leg to get it out of the way of the rising tail of the board. If he times this motion perfectly, his rear foot and the rear of the board rise in perfect unison, seemingly "stuck" together.

....

exerts: pushes **unison:** together
leveling out: making flat

From: "Frontside Forces and Fakie Flight: The Physics of Skateboarding Tricks." *Exploratorium.*
(www.exploratorium.edu/skateboarding/trick02.html)

NoteZone

Underline the three different objects that exert a force on the board when a skater performs an ollie.

FIND OUT MORE

SCIENCESAURUS

Balanced Forces 281
Unbalanced
 Forces 282
Newton's First
 Law of Motion 284

SCiLINKS
THE WORLD'S A CLICK AWAY

www.scilinks.org
Keyword: Force
Code: GSPD03

IDENTIFY THE FORCES

Study the diagram at right. The arrows show the direction and relative size of the different forces acting on the skateboard at the beginning of the ollie maneuver.

ground pushing up

gravity pulling down

▶ *Describe the forces acting on the board at this moment. In which direction are the forces acting? Which force is greater?*

_____

_____

_____

_____

_____

Newton's first law of motion says that objects at rest tend to stay at rest unless acted upon by an unbalanced force. It also says that objects in motion tend to stay in motion with the same speed and direction, unless acted upon by an unbalanced force.

▶ *What does Newton's first law say will happen when the force of the ground pushing up on the board is suddenly much greater than the force of gravity pulling down on the board?*

_____

_____

_____

_____

Newton's first law says that once the board lifts off the ground, it will continue moving upward unless it is acted upon by an unbalanced force.

▶ *What is the unbalanced force acting on the board that causes it to stop rising, change direction, and begin falling?*

_____

MAKE INFERENCES Think about what you have learned about the forces necessary to make a skateboard bounce into the air.

▶ *What do you think the skater could do to make the board go higher?*

_____

_____

_____

▶ *What would produce just a "baby" ollie?*

_____

_____

THINK ABOUT IT The ground pushes up on the tail of the skateboard only after the skater slams the tail down to hit the ground.

▶ *Think of another situation where slamming an object down to the ground causes the object to pop up into the air.*

_____

_____

Think about bouncing a basketball. To get the best bounce, you need plenty of air in the ball. You also need a good surface. A surface that will push back on the ball will provide the unbalanced force to send the ball back into the air.

▶ *Describe what makes a good surface for bouncing a basketball.*

_____

_____

_____

_____

▶ *Why do you suppose it would be much more difficult for a skater to do an ollie on soft ground instead of on pavement?*

_____

_____

_____

_____

May the Force Be With You

Mass Action

Discus throwing is both art and science.

Imagine tossing around a gallon jug of water. That's about the mass of the discus thrown by the ancient Greeks in Olympic competition, so don't confuse a discus with a Frisbee! The discus used by the ancient Greeks was a large, round, flat disc made of marble, bronze, or lead. They weren't all the same, but a typical discus may have had a mass anywhere between two and six kilograms. The discus throw was the first of five events in the Olympic pentathlon competition.

▶ **Read**

In the year 708 B.C., Lampis, a young athlete and discus thrower from the city-state of Sparta, came to test his strength and skill in the 18th Olympiad.

DISCUS THROW

Lampis waited patiently near the balbis. He carried a bronze discus on his shoulder. He rubbed the discus with fine sand so that he could get a firm grip. One of the contestants was about to complete his first discus throw. His body strained to bring the utmost force behind the throw. Lampis wondered whether the simple style of his rival, requiring only one step, might be more effective than his own, which needed three. Each contestant in the discus throw had five chances. A judge marked the best of the throws with a peg.

When his turn came, Lampis took his place on the balbis. His right foot was forward, bearing his weight. Holding the discus in his left hand, he let it swing forward and took it in his right. Then as the discus arced vigorously down and back, he bent his body to the right, turning his head so that he could see the right side of his body. Then, putting the whole force of his body into the movement, Lampis threw the discus. His throw was timed to the rhythm of flute music. The young Spartan saw the pegs set down by the judge and knew that he had done better than any of his competitors.

From: Glubock, Shirley and Alfred Tamarin. *Olympic Games in Ancient Greece.* HarperCollins.

balbis: the sloped platform the discus was thrown from

bronze: a metal made of a mixture of copper and tin

utmost: greatest

rival: opponent

effective: powerful

arced: swung in a circular path

vigorously: quickly

Explore

FLYING FARTHER Newton's first law explains that an object that is not moving will not start moving until an unbalanced force acts on it.

▶ *What unbalanced force acted on Lampis's discus to make it start moving?*

_____

Newton's second law explains the relationship between the unbalanced forces acting on an object, the mass of the object, and the acceleration of the object that results. (Acceleration is a measure of how quickly the speed or direction of an object is changing.) Newton came up with the equation $F = m \times a$ to explain how these three factors are related.

Use Newton's equation to calculate the acceleration of a discus in each of the following cases:

A *force of*	will give a *mass of*	an *acceleration of*
16 Newtons	4 kg	_____ m/s^2
12 Newtons	4 kg	_____ m/s^2
8 Newtons	4 kg	_____ m/s^2
4 Newtons	4 kg	_____ m/s^2

▶ *How would using more force change the acceleration of the discus? (Use the data in the chart on page 25 to find the answer.)*

_____

_____

The greater the acceleration of the discus, the greater its speed will be when it leaves the thrower's hand.

▶ *How would using more force change the speed of the discus as it is thrown?*

_____

_____

Finally, the greater the speed of a discus when it leaves the hand of the thrower, the farther it will travel.

▶ *How would using more force change the distance the discus flies?*

_____

_____

MAKE COMPARISONS The discus used by the ancient Greeks varied from one competition to another. The mass might be 1.5 kg or 4.5 kg. But for any one contest, all athletes used the same discus.

▶ *Use Newton's second law to explain why this would be important for a fair competition.*

_____

_____

_____

_____

Today, a typical discus is made of wood instead of marble or bronze, and has metal only around the rim. The mass of today's standard Olympic discus is 2 kg.

▶ *If Lampis competed in the discus throw today, what do you think his reaction might be when he first picked up a modern wood discus?*

_____

_____

26

WRITE A LIMERICK

A limerick is a five-line poem. The first, second, and fifth lines rhyme with each other and have about nine syllables per line. The third and fourth lines rhyme with each other and have five or six syllables each. The following limerick was written about Newton's second law.

> Said Sir Isaac: "I've got a great notion
> That force is a changer of motion.
> Let's put it this way:
> F equals *ma*
> The rest is just sweat and devotion."
> — A. P. French

Use this limerick as a model to write your own limerick about Newton's second law.

▶ *Start by listing terms that relate to the second law, then think of words that rhyme with those terms.*

▲ **Sir Isaac Newton**

_____

_____

_____

_____

_____

_____

▶ *Next, write a limerick.*

_____

_____

_____

_____

_____

_____

May the Force Be With You

Rocket Reaction

What does it take to make a rocket soar?

What could a balloon possibly have in common with a rocket? Plenty! Both would flop without Newton's third law of motion.

Read

Homer Hickam is 14 years old. His teacher, Miss Riley, has brought Homer and his model rocket to see the school principal.

Rocket Boy

"The McDowell County Science Fair is in March. Miss Riley believes you should be allowed to represent the school.... Are you prepared to answer tough questions?"

"Yes, sir."

"All right then.... What makes a rocket fly?"

"Newton's third law. For every action, there is an equal and opposite reaction."

He stabbed the drawing of the nozzle. "And this peculiar shape? What's it for?"

"That is a DeLaval nozzle. It's designed to convert slow-moving, high-pressure gases into a stream of low-pressure, high-velocity gases. If the gases reach a sonic velocity at the throat, they will go supersonic in the diverging part of the nozzle, producing maximum thrust."

"You taught him all this, Miss Riley?"

"No, he taught it to himself."

---

nozzle: narrow opening
convert: change
velocity: speed
sonic: traveling at the speed of sound

supersonic: traveling faster than the speed of sound
diverging: widening
thrust: push

From: Hickam, Homer H. *Rocket Boys*. Delacorte Press.

Activity

WATCH IT FLY

Build your own balloon rocket.

What You Need: one small balloon

What to Do:

1. Blow up the balloon and pinch the neck closed.
2. In an open area, hold the balloon horizontally and then release it.
3. Observe what happens to the balloon.

WHAT DO YOU SEE?

▶ *What happened to the balloon when you let go of the neck? Draw the balloon as it looked right before and right after you let go of the neck. Use an arrow to show what direction the balloon moved.*

▶ *What two things are moving in the second part of your drawing? (Hint: What comes out of the balloon?)*

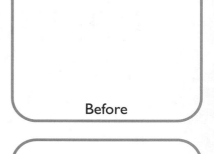

Before

After

Propose Explanations

IDENTIFY FORCES Newton's third law says that for every action there is an equal and opposite reaction. That means that every time one object exerts a force on another object, the second object exerts an equal force back on the first object.

▶ *Can you identify the two opposite forces in your balloon diagram?*

_____

_____

▶ *Identify the two opposite actions in your balloon diagram.*

_____

_____

▶ *How is your balloon like Homer's rocket?*

_____

_____

_____

Da Vinci's Designs

CURIOUS MINDS

Five hundred years ago, an Italian artist sketched designs for dozens of fantastic machines.

Leonardo da Vinci was born in Florence, Italy, in 1452. Leonardo worked as a painter, draftsman, sculptor, architect, and engineer. He is remembered mainly as an artist, but Leonardo's notebooks show that he worked constantly to gain new knowledge as a scientist. He wrote notes and drew sketches of things in his world that interested him (almost everything!). He also drew pictures of his ideas for inventions of new machines.

▲ **Leonardo da Vinci**

 **Before You Read**

RECOGNIZING SIMPLE MACHINES A machine is a tool you use to make work easier. Machines can be very complex, but there are a few machines that are called *simple machines*. Simple machines make work easier by changing the size or direction of a force. These machines were used for many centuries, even before Leonardo's time.

▶ *Have you ever seen any of these simple machines in use, either by themselves or as part of another machine? Write down any examples you can think of. Describe what the machine does.*

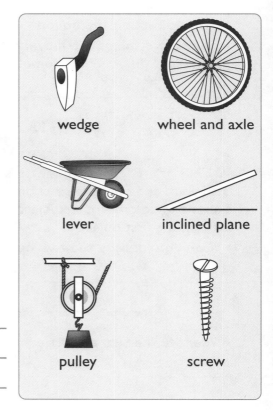

wedge   wheel and axle

lever   inclined plane

pulley   screw

_____

_____

_____

_____

_____

_____

 **Read**

NOTEZONE

What else would you like to know about Leonardo's work after reading this excerpt?

As an apprentice, Leonardo spent lots of time taking apart machines in order to understand them better.

INVENTOR'S WORKSHOP

Leonardo's fascination with machines probably began during his boyhood. Some of his earliest sketches clearly show how various machine parts worked. As an apprentice [to a famous artist], Leonardo observed and used a variety of machines. By studying them he gained practical knowledge about their design and structure.

Many ancient machines were in common use in Leonardo's time. For example, water wheels turned millstones to grind grain and Archimedes' screws lifted water from streams providing a ready supply for drinking and washing.

Artists and craftsmen in Leonardo's time knew how to build and repair the familiar kinds of machines. The idea of inventing new kinds of machines, however, would not have occurred to [many of] them.

Leonardo developed a unique new attitude about machines. He reasoned that by understanding how each separate machine part worked, he could modify them and combine them in different ways to improve existing machines or create inventions no one had ever seen before.

Leonardo set out to write the first systematic explanations of how machines work and how the elements of machines can be combined.

fascination: great interest
apprentice: a person who works for an expert to learn a trade or skill
millstones: circular stones

Archimedes' screw: machine used to lift water
unique: one of a kind
systematic: orderly

From: "Inventor's Workshop." *The Museum of Science.*
(www.mos.org/sln/Leonardo/InventorsWorkshop.html)

FIND OUT MORE

SCIENCESAURUS

Simple Machines	288
Inclined Plane	289
Wedge	290
Screw	291
Lever	292
Wheel and Axle	293
Pulley	294

SCiLINKS
THE WORLD'S A CLICK AWAY

www.scilinks.com
Keyword: Simple Machines
Code: GSPD04

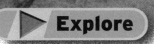
PICTURE THIS! Leonardo took apart plants, animals, and machines in order to be able to draw them realistically. He also drew the things he saw in order to be able to understand them. Here is a sketch of a machine that probably was used in Leonardo's time to haul water up out of a well.

▶ *Review simple machines in your textbook or your ScienceSaurus handbook. Use your book to help you find the simple machines that make up this one. Use arrows to label each simple machine you find.*

_____

_____

▶ *Write what you think the role of each labeled part is. Use information from your reference book to help you.*

_____

_____

_____

_____

_____

_____

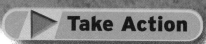

WRITE A PARAGRAPH Leonardo was a painter who learned to build his own canvases and mix his own paints. He was a sculptor who learned to build the molds needed to cast bronze statues. By taking apart and studying the parts of living and nonliving things, Leonardo was able to understand how things work. Accurate drawings helped him record what he had learned so that he could review the information later.

People who make major new discoveries are often people who put *ideas* together in new ways, not just things. How do you think being interested in many different subjects made it possible for Leonardo to come up with ideas for building three of his most famous inventions: a flying machine, a parachute, and an underwater breathing machine? What ideas or observations might have led him to these inventions?

_____

_____

_____

_____

_____

_____

_____

People often have new ideas that they don't pay attention to because they think the ideas might be silly. Try to remember any interesting ideas you might have had for a new machine, but ignored. Describe one of your ideas below.

_____

_____

_____

_____

_____

_____

_____

Da Vinci's Designs

Gadget Gawking

You can try out Leonardo's methods for understanding how machines work.

Leonardo da Vinci wanted to understand how compound machines work, so he took them apart. He studied the pieces and sketched what he saw. The most basic parts of a compound machine are simple machines. By finding out how the simple machines worked, Leonardo was able to put them together in new ways to make new machines.

 **Activity**

SKETCH A GADGET

What You Need: drawing paper, pencils, erasers, a compound machine (such as a rotary eggbeater, a handheld can opener, a rotary drill, a hand wrench, a mechanical pencil sharpener, or a bicycle)

What to Do:
1. Choose a compound machine and study it carefully. Watch how each part moves and try to identify any simple machines.
2. Sketch the machine while it is not moving. Also make separate sketches to show the details of any small parts.
3. Draw other pictures of your machine from different views to show all the working parts.
4. Add arrows to your sketches to show the direction in which each part moves.

SCILINKS
THE WORLD'S A CLICK AWAY

www.scilinks.org
Keyword: Simple
Machines
Code: GSPD04

Refer to your textbook or your *ScienceSaurus* handbook to help you label the simple machines you found in this compound machine.

▷ Propose Explanations

PUTTING IT TOGETHER What is the function of the compound-machine gadget you examined?

_____

_____

Refer to the drawings in Lesson 7 on page 30 to help you recognize the simple machines in this compound machine.

▶ *What is the role of each simple machine in this gadget?*

_____

_____

▶ *How do the various parts work together to accomplish the task of the compound machine?*

_____

_____

▶ Take Action

BE AN INVENTOR Be an inventor for a day. Imagine a new compound-machine gadget that would make your life easier. For example, can you invent a machine to make your bed? Before you begin, review the ways that each simple machine can be used to make work easier. How could you combine two or more simple machines to increase their usefulness?

Sketch your invention in the box. Identify the simple machines that you combined. Then explain what your machine does and how it works.

_____

_____

_____

_____

_____

Da Vinci's Designs

LEO'S MACHINES TODAY

Leonardo's inventions were hundreds of years ahead of their time.

The first time someone jumped from a high place using a parachute was in France in 1783. Armies used tanks for the first time during World War I in 1917. The first airplane with landing gear that folded up came out in 1933. Yet, all these ideas were sketched in detail by Leonardo da Vinci in the late 1400s and early 1500s.

 **Read**

See how Leonardo's sketches compare to similar modern machines.

Visions of the Future

Leonardo described and sketched ideas for many inventions hundreds of years ahead of their time. But it seems [that] very few of these were ever built and tested during his life. Though his notes suggest that he wished to organize and publish his ideas, he died before he could accomplish this important goal. After his death, his notebooks were hidden away, scattered, or lost, and his wonderful ideas were forgotten.

Centuries passed before other inventors came up with similar ideas and brought them to practical use.

[Here are two] modern inventions [that] Leonardo envisioned...in his notebooks over 500 years ago.

Leonardo sketched several different designs for flying machines including this one [at the right] with a rotating [propeller]. He intended to power it with a wound-up spring.

[The picture on the left] is a U.S. Navy helicopter capable of carrying heavy loads. The first helicopter that could carry a person was designed and flown [with a gasoline-powered engine] by Paul Cornu in 1907....

Leonardo sketched designs for several different diving suits. Most required a diver to breathe air from the surface through long hoses. In this design, he imagined a crush proof air chamber attached to the diver's chest to allow the diver to swim freely without connection to the surface.

Modern SCUBA divers can swim freely underwater while breathing compressed air from tanks on their backs. Jacques-Yves Cousteau and Emile Gagnon invented [the] self-contained breathing apparatus [shown at left,] in 1943.

envisioned: pictured
capable: able
SCUBA: Self-Contained Underwater Breathing Apparatus

compressed: squeezed together
apparatus: equipment

From: "Visions of the Future." *The Museum of Science.*
(www.mos.org/sln/Leonardo/InventorsWorkshop.html)

NOTEZONE

For each pair of pictures, draw lines to connect parts of Leonardo's invention to similar parts of the modern machine.

FIND OUT MORE

SCIENCESAURUS

Simple Machines 288
History of Science
Time Line 440

SCILINKS
THE WORLD'S A CLICK AWAY

www.scilinks.org
Keyword: Simple Machines
Code: GSPD04

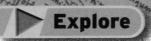

Explore

MAKE COMPARISONS

▶ *How is Leonardo da Vinci's design for a helicopter similar to a modern-day helicopter? How is it different?*

_____

_____

_____

_____

_____

▶ *How is Leonardo's design for an underwater breathing machine similar to the one invented in 1943? How is it different?*

_____

_____

_____

_____

THINK ABOUT IT Leonardo drew sketches of many inventions that weren't actually built until centuries later. One of those is the parachute, which he drew sketches of in the late 1400s.

▶ *Why do you suppose people of his time might not have recognized this as a useful invention? (Hint: Think about how parachutes are used today.)*

_____

_____

_____

When the Wright brothers were working on building the first airplane in the 1890s and early 1900s, most people thought they were just foolish. Even after the first successful flight, few people were impressed.

▶ *How do you suppose people in the 1400s probably reacted to Leonardo's idea for a helicopter?*

_____

_____

_____

38

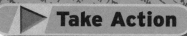
MACHINES THEN AND NOW Many machines that we use today had previous versions that were different. Some older machines, such as rotary eggbeaters, look much as they did many years ago. Others, such as bicycles, look different.

Interview an adult to learn about some old machines. Find out what has changed from the old machine to the new machine. How is the new machine better? Can it do more? What are its advantages over the older version? How does the new machine make life easier? Are there any disadvantages with the new version? Record the results of your interview below.

Machine

_____

How the Machine Has Changed

_____
_____
_____
_____
_____
_____
_____

How the New Machine Makes Life Easier

_____
_____
_____
_____
_____
_____
_____

Modern Machines

Robot Ants

Some robots are not much bigger than your thumb.

Ants live together in large groups called colonies. Ants in colonies work together to get big jobs done quickly. Perhaps you've seen a group of ants marching in a line between a food source and their nest. When engineer James McLurkin was a college student at the Massachusetts Institute of Technology, he studied how ant colonies cooperate. Then he used this knowledge about nature to develop new machines that cooperate.

▲ **James McLurkin**

▶ **Read**

FIND OUT MORE

SCIENCESAURUS
Steps in Technology
Design   357
Military and Space
Technology   366

SCiLINKS
THE WORLD'S A CLICK AWAY

www.scilinks.org
Keyword: Robots
Code: GSPD05

James McLurkin created a colony of tiny robot ants.

An Idea from Nature

They can go around obstacles, look for food and even play tag. They're programmed to behave like ants in a colony, but they're not insects—they're matchbook-sized robots....

Each [robot ant] has a pair of tiny treads powered by a battery and two motors.... The robots are guided away from objects they hit and toward [light] sources by antennae and light sensors. [T]hey also have mandibles powered by a third motor to pick up bits of "food"—quarter-inch balls [0.5 cm] of crumpled brass.

Mr. McLurkin's goal is to have the robots behave cooperatively like an ant colony, [looking for] food and communicating with each other about where to find it. They do this with the aid of infrared transmitters and receivers (similar to those used by television remote controls) and software. If one robot finds food, it sends out the message "I found food." [O]thers in the [area] that receive [the signal] respond by heading toward the sender and signaling "I found a robot that found food." [In this way, they] eventually spread...the word to the entire group....

© GREAT SOURCE. COPYING IS PROHIBITED.

So goes the theory. In practice, Mr. McLurkin has found that the robots...get confused if they receive signals from more than four other robots at once....

obstacles: objects in the way

treads: heavy rubber belts that act as tires

antennae: feelers used to sense the environment

light sensors: instruments that respond to light

mandibles: jaws

infrared transmitters: instruments that send out signals

receivers: instruments that take in signals

software: part of a computer that processes information

theory: idea

From: Waugh, Alice. "MIT Senior's Robot Begets 'Ant' Farm." *MIT News.* (web.mit.edu/newsoffice/nr/1995/40009.html)

Explore

COMPARING ANTS Using the excerpt and the ant diagram, find and label the following parts of the robotic ant: mandibles, treads, and antennae.

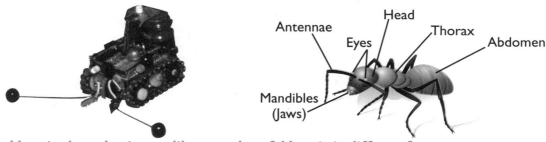

► *How is the robotic ant like a real ant? How is it different?*

_____

_____

_____

► *How are the robotic ants like an ant colony? How are they different?*

_____

_____

_____

► *How might being able to communicate with one another make the robotic ants more useful as robots?*

_____

_____

Modern Machines

Milking Machines

A machine can get the milk out of a cow, and the farmer doesn't even have to be there.

Do you have milk with your cereal? Do you butter your toast? Do you eat ice cream? Have you ever had a grilled cheese sandwich? If your answer to any of these questions is yes, you can thank the people who milk dairy cows twice a day, seven days a week, 365 days a year. The cows produce milk all the time, and so they have to be milked on time, all the time. Milking machines have existed for years, but getting them on and off the cows is tedious and time-consuming work.

Recently, engineers have invented a new kind of milking machine. It is still very expensive, but before long it might make the lives of many dairy farmers a whole lot easier.

▶ Before You Read

THE OLD-FASHIONED WAY Many machines you use every day do jobs that were once done by people. For example, bread-making machines automatically knead and bake bread. An automatic car wash can clean the outside of the car while you relax inside.

▶ *What other machines do jobs that people once did? If you're not sure, ask an older person. List the machines below, along with the job they do and a brief explanation of how the job used to be done.*

_____

_____

_____

_____

_____

_____

_____

_____

UNIT 1: MOTION AND FORCES

 **Read**

NOTEZONE

Underline four parts of the robotic milking machine.

Can dairy cows be trained to milk themselves?

Robots in the Dairy Barn

The dairy farms of Europe are as [charming] as ever, but for the past 10 years they've had something American farms lack: robotic milking technology. Labor costs are higher [in Europe], so as many as half the European dairies have the machines, which can milk cows 24 hours a day with no human [contact].... Lately, American farmers have begun to wonder if the machines...are worth a try....

With the right equipment, cows can be trained to milk themselves. They are [led in]to the machine with food, but soon learn to go there whenever their udders are full. When a cow enters the milking station, a computer scans an [identification] tag on her collar (1). A robotic arm swings under her udder (2) and washes it. A laser locates the exact position of her teats, attaches four [milking] cups (3), and starts milking. Milk from each teat is measured by a computer that releases the cups when milk flow stops. The robotic arm disinfects the udder, swings back (4), and the cow exits (5).

robotic: automatic
technology: equipment
udders: the sacs on cows that hold milk
laser: narrow beam of light
teats: parts of the udder that milk comes out of
disinfects: cleans off germs that might cause disease

From: Lanigan, Diane. "With the Right Equipment, Cows Can Be Trained to Milk Themselves." *Popular Science Newsfiles.* (www.popsci.com/popsci/science/article/0,12543,265562,00.html)

FIND OUT MORE

SCIENCESAURUS

Steps in Technology
  Design   357
Limits on Technology
  Design   358
Natural Limits on
  Technology   359
Economic Limits
  on Technology 360
Society and
  Research   364
Society's Values 365
Tradeoffs   369
Reasonable People
  Disagree   373

SCILINKS
THE WORLD'S A CLICK AWAY

www.scilinks.org
Keyword: Robots
Code: GSPD05

An earlier milking machine ▶

DECODE A DIAGRAM The diagram shows the steps in milking a cow with a robotic milking machine. Compare the diagram to the description in the reading.

▶ *What human action is replaced by each of the numbered steps in the diagram?*

1 _____

2 _____

3 _____

4 _____

5 _____

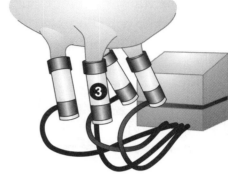

A FARMER'S LIFE Dairy farmers have a hard time taking a day off. Dairy cows must be milked twice a day on a regular basis. If they are not, they will stop producing milk. The work is hard and one person can't do it alone. Recently, many people who own small dairy farms have decided that it is just not possible to make a living as a farmer. Too much hard work and not enough profit make them want to give up. But some people think that robotic milking machines might make it possible for more families to keep their small dairy farms.

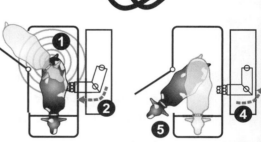

▶ *Old milking machines were operated by people. It used to take about five minutes to milk one cow. If a farmer had 50 cows, how long did it take to milk them all?*

_____

▶ *How much time did he spend milking each day if he milked the whole herd twice a day?*

_____

▶ *How might a robotic milking machine make a dairy farmer's life easier?*

_____

_____

_____

_____

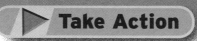

DEBATE THE ISSUE Within every group of people, you will find differences of opinion. One way that people share different ideas is through a debate. A debate is not an argument. Each side is allowed to present its position without being disturbed. Then questions are asked and answered in order to explore the issue further.

Hold a debate about the advantages and disadvantages of having machines do jobs that people used to do.

What You Need:
- index cards

What to Do:
1. Form a team with classmates.
2. Begin by reviewing the list of machines you made on page 42.
3. Write the name of each machine on an index card. For each machine, decide what its advantages (or disadvantages) are and write them on the card. For example, an advantage might be "The machine gives people more free time." A disadvantage might be "The machine causes pollution."
4. With your teammates, develop a list of points to make to present your position on each machine. If necessary, do additional research to find new points.
5. Hold a debate with the other side by taking turns making your case about each machine.
6. As the other team makes its case, write down any additional questions you want to ask them.
7. Ask the other team your side's questions. They will do the same with your team.

Write Reflections
What did you learn from the debate? Did the arguments you heard make you change your mind about anything? If so, what?

_____

_____

_____

_____

_____

_____

_____

Modern Machines

Transporting Humans

Imagine moving down the sidewalk without an ounce of effort!

▲ **Dean Kamen**

Throughout history, inventors have taken existing machines and ideas, added their own ideas, and created new machines. One idea inventors are always trying to improve upon is how to more easily transport objects and people from one place to another. The wheel was invented thousands of years ago. But inventors are still working on new ways to use it today!

One of those inventors is Dean Kamen. He has created the Segway—a machine designed to carry one person along the sidewalk.

▶ **Before You Read**

BEAM ME UP Movies, television shows, comics, and books often show us what the future might look like, especially in terms of technology. Science-fiction writers have come up with fascinating ideas for how to transport individual people easily from one place to another.

What unusual or original method have you seen for transporting humans? How did it work? Where could it take people? If you can't think of any you have seen, what would you like to invent? Write about an imaginary human transportation system in the space below.

_____

_____

_____

_____

_____

_____

_____

_____

_____

▶ Read

NOTEZONE

What else do you want to know about Segway after reading this?

Inventor Dean Kamen wants to improve the way we get around with a new machine.

Make Way for Segway!

Segway looks like a cross between a scooter and a lawnmower. The battery-powered scooter travels as fast as 17 miles per hour and has internal gyroscopes that make it difficult to fall from or knock over. A gyroscope is a wheel-like device that maintains its steady position no matter how it is moved.

Segway's coolest feature may be that its speed and direction are controlled by the rider's shifting weight. Riders navigate with a bicycle-like handlebar. By simply standing up straight, the scooter takes you wherever you want to go. It doesn't have brakes, but is smart enough to sense when the rider wants to stop....

Kamen is already famous for a variety of inventions including a wheelchair that climbs stairs. The New Hampshire-based inventor hopes Segway will one day be used on city sidewalks, where riders won't need a license. He also hopes his latest invention will replace cars in big cities and help the environment by cutting down on car use and pollution.

device: piece of equipment
navigate: steer

From: El Nabli, Dina. "Make Way for Segway!" *Time for Kids.*
(www.timeforkids.com/TFK/news/printout/0,9187,187023,00.html)

The Segway ▶

COMPARE BICYCLES AND SEGWAYS The bicycle is a familiar machine for moving people. You can probably name all the bicycle's main parts: frame, seat, handlebars, pedals, chain, gears, brakes.

The important parts of the Segway are a bit harder to see. The Segway has two electric motors powered by batteries. The motors are connected to large plastic wheels with rubber tires. Each wheel can spin by itself. The two wheels can turn in different directions at the same time. Because of this the machine can turn in a complete circle without moving forward or backward. Special sensors keep track of the rider's position. The rider's position tells the motors how the rider wants to move. A twist grip on the handlebars allows the rider to steer. A red button allows the rider to stop the machine.

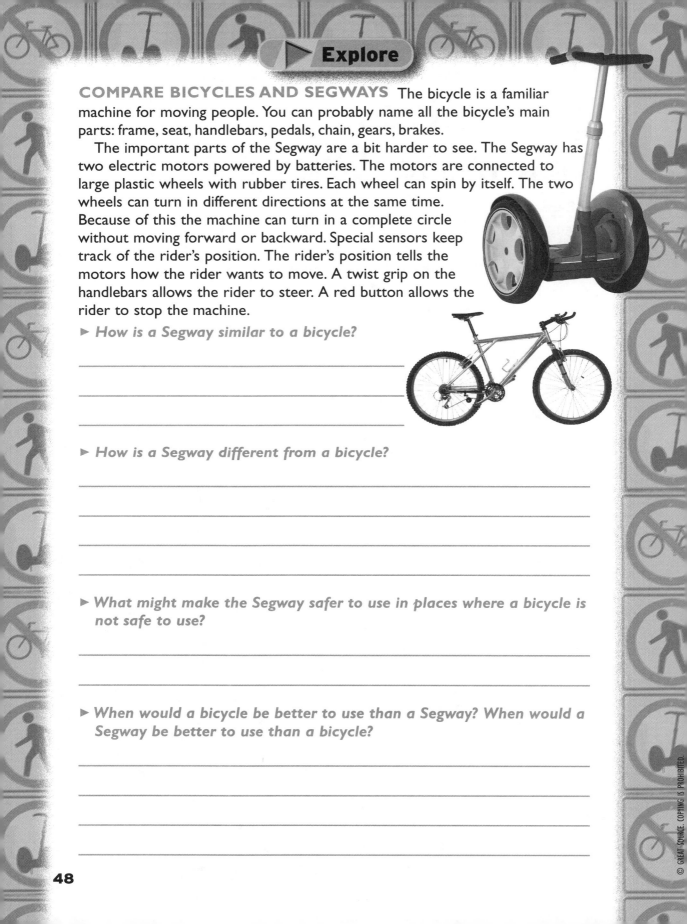

▶ *How is a Segway similar to a bicycle?*

_____

_____

_____

▶ *How is a Segway different from a bicycle?*

_____

_____

_____

_____

▶ *What might make the Segway safer to use in places where a bicycle is not safe to use?*

_____

_____

▶ *When would a bicycle be better to use than a Segway? When would a Segway be better to use than a bicycle?*

_____

_____

_____

_____

NOTHING'S PERFECT When you see a transporter in a science-fiction movie, it seems like a perfect machine. It does a great job and doesn't cause any problems. Real life inventions are not so perfect. They have limitations—characteristics that make them less useful than their inventors hoped.

▶ *What limitations does the Segway have? List at least three. Look back at the picture on page 48 for ideas.*

_____

_____

_____

_____

_____

▶ *What might be a solution to one of these limitations?*

_____

_____

_____

_____

_____

▶ Take Action

FIND OUT MORE Dean Kamen sees his invention being ridden on sidewalks in cities. Not everyone agrees that this is a good idea. List all the vehicles you have seen on sidewalks. Include those with motors and without motors—for example, scooters and motorized scooters. Contact the police department in your town or a nearby city. Find out which of these vehicles are allowed on sidewalks today. Based on what you learn, write whether you think the Segway would be allowed. Explain your prediction.

_____

_____

_____

_____

_____

UNIT 2
Electricity and Magnetism

Is it nature or technology?

Electricity is a form of energy, and magnetism is a force. Both are found in nature. And both have been harnessed by people for their own uses. Remember that the energy that powers your TV, telephone, and computer is the very same kind of energy that creates enormous bolts of lightning across the sky. Magnetic materials can be found in the rocks that make up Earth, but they can also be used to produce electricity and to make train travel more efficient.

In this unit you will learn about how magnetism is related to electricity. You'll explore the causes of static electricity and the origin of the electric light bulb. You'll learn the role of Earth's magnetic field in two mysterious happenings in nature. And you'll discover how everyday devices like computers depend on the precise control of electricity.

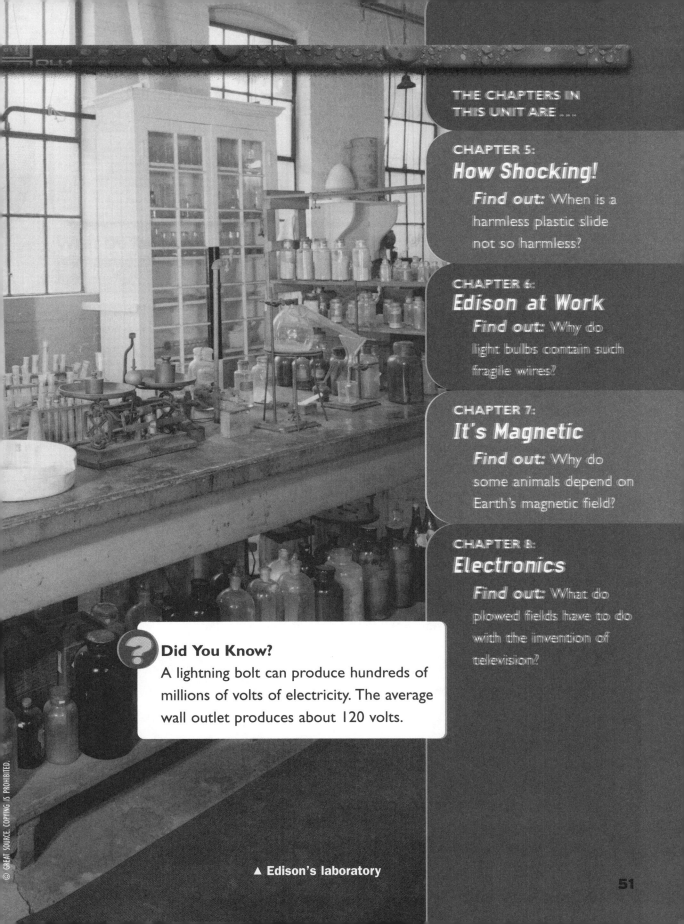

? **Did You Know?**
A lightning bolt can produce hundreds of
millions of volts of electricity. The average
wall outlet produces about 120 volts.

▲ **Edison's laboratory**

How Shocking!

ZAP ATTACK!

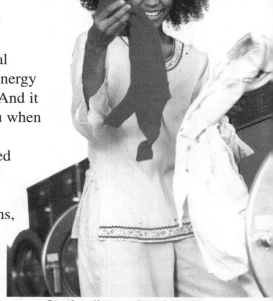

Static electricity is everywhere. Are you shocked?

Have you ever felt a shock when you touched a metal doorknob after walking across a carpet? That same energy can also make your hair hard to comb in the winter. And it can make your clothes cling to each other and to you when they come out of the dryer.

This annoying energy comes from something called electric charge. Everything in the world is chock full of particles with charge, either positive or negative. The particles with negative charge are called electrons, and the ones with positive charge are called protons. Any two opposite charges pull toward each other, but any two like charges try to push apart. When a huge number of like charges are all forced onto one object with no escape route, the result is called static charge, or static electricity.

▲ **Static cling makes laundry stick together.**

▶ Before You Read

OUCH! Even when you know it's coming, a shock from static electricity feels like a surprise, and it is always a little unpleasant. Sometimes the jolt catches you completely off guard, and sometimes it really hurts.

▶ *Think of a time when you got an electric shock. Describe the situation. Can you remember what the weather was like?*

_____

_____

_____

▶ *Have you ever shocked another person? Described what happened.*

_____

_____

_____

_____

▶ Read

Read about how children might get a "charge" out of playing on a plastic slide.

The Zapper Slide

Can [enough] static charge build [up on] plastic playground equipment to harm someone?

Static electricity can build up when materials such as plastic are rubbed. The <mark>friction</mark> involved in the rubbing can either remove <mark>electrons</mark> from the plastic leaving the plastic positively charged or add extra electrons onto the plastic leaving it negatively charged....

Let's take a slide as an example of the [plastic] playground equipment.... As [a] child slides down the slide, [his or her] clothes will rub on the plastic and a [static] charge could...build up on both the child and the slide.

Is this charge enough to hurt someone? Ask Peter Ledlie, a father playing on a plastic slide with his daughter:

...It was during a warm day here in Phoenix, (85 deg[rees F]) [29.4 degrees C] with humidity around 15 [percent]. I went on a plastic slide, and could feel and hear the charges building up as I went down. I put my hands out at the end to stop, and brushed by one of the [metal] bolts, getting a painful zap!

---

friction: force created by rubbing
electrons: negatively charged particles

From: "Can a Static Charge [on] Plastic Playground Equipment ... Harm Someone?" *ScienceNet Quick Links.* (www.sciencenet.org.uk/database/Biology/0107/b00982d.html)

Fowler, Steve. "Are Children's Slides at Fast Food Restaurants a Static Hazard?" *ESD Journal.* (www.esdjournal.com/static/believeit/slides/slides.htm)

FIND OUT MORE

SCIENCESAURUS
Atomic Structure 256
The Law of
  Electric Charges 315
Static Electricity 316

SCI LINKS.
THE WORLD'S A CLICK AWAY

www.scilinks.org
Keyword: Static
  Electricity
Code: GSPD06

HOW DID PETER LEDLIE GET ZAPPED?

As Peter Ledlie came down the slide, charges built up on him and on the slide.

▶ *What made this happen?*

_____

_____

_____

Below is a diagram of Peter Ledlie on the slide. Add plus (+) and minus (−) signs to show positive and negative charges built up on Peter and on the slide. (Hint: There may be more than one correct way to do this.)

A shock is felt when static discharge occurs. Static discharge occurs when a charged object touches another object and the built-up charges move quickly off the charged object. The charges move most quickly when the object touched is a conductor—a material that charges move through easily. Metal is a good conductor.

▶ *On the diagram, circle the spot where the discharge took place.*

▶ *If there hadn't been a metal bolt on the side of the slide, do you think Peter Ledlie would have gotten shocked? Explain your answer.*

_____

_____

_____

ZAPPING STATIC

Can dryer sheets help you avoid "the shock"?

What You Need:
- very small pieces of paper
- blown-up balloons
- small piece of wool
- dryer sheets

What to Do:
1. Make a pile of very small bits of paper on your desk.
2. Rub one side of a balloon with a piece of wool for about 30 seconds.
3. Pass that part of the balloon over the pieces of paper. Write your observations in the chart.
4. Now rub one side of the wool with the dryer sheet for about 30 seconds. Then use that side of the wool to rub another balloon in the same way as the first balloon.
5. Pass that part of the balloon over the pieces of paper again. Write your observations in the chart.

What Do You See?

	Observations
Balloon rubbed with wool	
Balloon rubbed with dryer-sheet-treated wool	

What Happened?

► *Describe what happened in steps two and three in terms of "built-up charges."*

_____

_____

► *What can you infer about how the dryer sheet affected the build-up of charges on the wool and the balloon?*

_____

_____

► *How might you be able to stop the "zap attack" of a plastic slide?*

_____

_____

_____

How Shocking!

HOT DOG

Scientists think lightning may strike somewhere on Earth a hundred times each second.

Lightning is a form of static electricity. Like the shock you sometimes get after walking across a carpeted room, lightning is caused by the sudden release of positive or negative charges that have built up on an object. As you might have guessed, however, a lightning bolt is a lot more powerful than a carpet shock.

◄ Sport survived, but the house was damaged as shown above and below this doorway

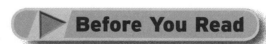

Before You Read

LIGHTNING STRIKES Lightning can be frightening, and it is dangerous. Fortunately, it's not too hard to predict when lightning is likely to happen. People can stay safe by staying indoors at those times.

► *When have you seen lightning? Did the lightning strike anything? What was the effect?*

_____

_____

_____

_____

► *What did the lightning look like? Where did it seem to begin and where did it appear to go?*

_____

_____

_____

UNIT 2: ELECTRICITY AND MAGNETISM

▶ **Read**

NOTEZONE

Underline the effect that lightning had on objects on the ground.

One day lightning struck the house of Sally Andis. Afterwards, she discovered something so strange that she told the local newspaper about it.

Dog OK after Lightning Hits

WASHINGTON, Ind. — A dog hit by lightning that struck a tree and traveled through the chain that had been holding him escaped with singed fur and a wounded paw, but no serious injuries.

After Sally Andis saw the bolt hit a tree near her rural southwestern Indiana home on Wednesday night, the dog was nowhere to be seen. The lightning broke the chain, and the heat burned a ring around the tree where the chain had been fastened. Four black paw prints were left on concrete outside the home's back door, where the dog, a beagle named Sport, had been standing.

When Ms. Andis found the dog, his fur was singed and his body felt hot. He was panting and bleeding from one paw. A trip to the veterinarian assured the family that Sport will be OK, but Ms. Andis told the Washington Times-Herald that the dog no longer wants to leave her side.

▲ Sport left blackened paw prints on the concrete where he was standing when lightning struck.

The family's house, about eight miles south of Washington, didn't fare so well. The lightning blew bricks 30 to 40 feet [9 to 12 meters] out of the home's foundation and damaged a door frame. Every appliance in the house had its cord blown out of the outlets, and the bolt left smoke outside and inside the house.

....

singed: slightly burned
rural: in the country
fastened: attached
assured: told

fare: do
foundation: the solid base on which a house is built

From: "Dog OK After Lightning Hits." *The Associated Press.*

FIND OUT MORE

SCIENCESAURUS
The Law of
Electric Charges 315
Static Electricity 316

THE WORLD'S A CLICK AWAY

www.scilinks.org
Keyword: Static
 Electricity
Code: GSPD06

WHAT MAKES LIGHTNING STRIKE? Normally, clouds contain an even mix of negative and positive charges. During a rainstorm, however, positive charges move up to the tops of tall clouds. As a result, an overall negative charge is produced at the bottom of the clouds.

Remember that like charges repel each other. Positive charges push other positive charges away. Negative charges push other negative charges away. In this way, charges in the bottom of clouds can affect the charges that build up on objects beneath them—including the ground.

The following diagram shows storm clouds forming above a house and tree. Using the information you just learned, label the diagram to show what charges, positive (+) or negative (−), are building up in the tops and bottoms of the clouds. Then infer what charges would be building up on the tree and on the ground beneath the clouds.

Opposite charges in the clouds and on the ground want to move toward each other. But the charges do not move easily through air. So the charges try to follow the shortest, easiest path through the air.

▶ *What object in Sally Andis's yard did the lightning hit? Use what you just learned to explain why this might have happened.*

_____

_____

_____

If you are unexpectedly caught outside in a lightning storm, experts advise that you get into a "lightning position."

▶ *Describe what you think the "lightning position" might be. How would it keep you as safe as possible?*

_____

_____

_____

ENERGY CHANGES All lightning starts out as electrical energy. But it is soon converted to other forms of energy.

▶ *Based on your experience and the reading, try to come up with four other forms of energy that electrical energy is converted to during a lightning strike. Draw a graphic organizer to show your ideas. Give evidence for all four of your answers.*

A lightning strike can raise the temperature of the air around it to 50,000°F (28,000°C)—five times hotter than the surface of the sun. Fortunately for Sport, the strike lasts only a fraction of a second.

▶ *What evidence did Sally Andis see that proved a lot of heat energy had been transferred to Sport?*

_____

_____

_____

Lightning causes about 10,000 forest fires in the United States each year.

▶ *How do you think lightning might start forest fires?*

_____

_____

_____

How Shocking!

Electric Eel

▲ **An electric eel**

The electric eel makes its own electricity in order to survive.

Electric eels are actually fresh-water fish that live in rivers in the Amazon rain forest. They can reach 3 meters (about 9 feet) in length and weigh more than 20 kilograms (about 44 pounds).

NOTEZONE

Underline what the electric eel uses to produce electricity.

▶ **Read**

One group of adventurers got a first-hand look at this very strange fish.

An Amazon Adventure

I heard the cry "Grab your camera and come see this!" One of the older fishermen of the area knew that we were interested in strange animals and had brought an electric eel that he had caught to the lodge....

The guides were encouraging people to touch the eel so they could feel the electric charge. When it was caught, it had discharged most of its energy and the guides were claiming that all you could feel was a slight tingling since it took some time for the animal to recharge. At full power, an electric eel has the ability to produce a charge...[strong] enough to stun or knock out a human or other large animal. Usually, the eels stun their prey and eat them when they can't move.

The charge is produced in [special] cells [called electroplates] found all along the tail of the animal. There are about 200 to 250 of these cells per centimeter of length. Larger eels...produce more energy [than smaller eels]. I declined the offer to touch it. ...I am not going to touch a big electric eel any more than I am going to stick my finger in a wall socket.

prey: an animal hunted by another

From: Frostick, Robert. *An Amazon Adventure—Electric Eel.* (jajhs.kana.k12.wv.us/amazon/eel.htm)

FIND OUT MORE

SCIENCESAURUS

The Law of
Electric Charges 315
Current Electricity 317
Electric Circuits 318

SCI LINKS
THE WORLD'S A CLICK AWAY

www.scilinks.org
Keyword: Static
Electricity
Code: GSPD06

UNIT 2: ELECTRICITY AND MAGNETISM

▷ Propose Explanations

WHAT'S THAT SHOCK? Each electroplate cell in the eel's body makes about 0.15 volts of electrical energy (about $\frac{1}{1000}$ the voltage from a wall outlet). These cells are lined up in long rows, like beads on a string. When the electroplates are all activated at once, the eel can discharge up to 600 volts of electrical energy. That's about 5 times the volts from an electrical wall outlet!

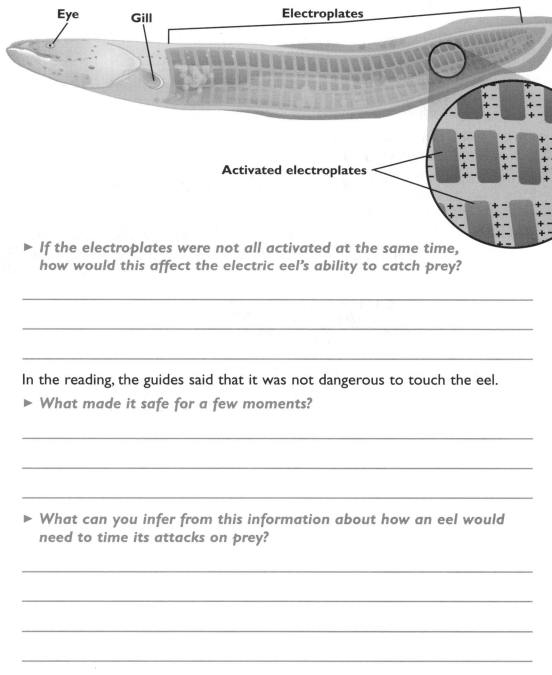

Eye   Gill   Electroplates

Activated electroplates

▶ *If the electroplates were not all activated at the same time, how would this affect the electric eel's ability to catch prey?*

_____

_____

_____

In the reading, the guides said that it was not dangerous to touch the eel.

▶ *What made it safe for a few moments?*

_____

_____

_____

▶ *What can you infer from this information about how an eel would need to time its attacks on prey?*

_____

_____

_____

_____

Edison at Work

Try, Try Again

How does someone become a great inventor? Does it take brains, hard work, or both?

Thomas Edison was one of the most famous men of his time. This creative genius patented more than 1,000 inventions. Edison is best known for his work on the incandescent light bulb and the phonograph, or record player. He even had a small studio for making silent films at his laboratory. Later, he figured out how to match sound with pictures, making it possible to create "talkies," movies with sound. Edison was often called the "Wizard of Menlo Park," named after his laboratories in Menlo Park, New Jersey.

The readings in this chapter come from the transcript of a television program *(Edison's Miracle of Light)* about Thomas Edison and the invention of the light bulb. A transcript is a written record of what people said. In this transcript, you will read what was said by the narrator of the TV program and by experts on Edison.

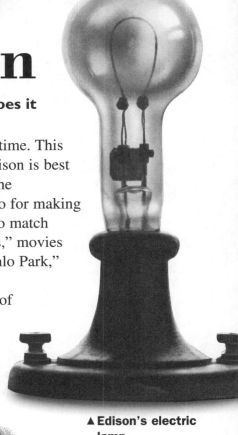

▲ Edison's electric lamp

▶ **Before You Read**

ELECTRICITY AT WORK Edison held 389 separate patents for inventions related to electric light and power. That's a lot of inventions!

▶ *Look around you and think about all the things you use that are powered by electricity. Make a list of ten electrical appliances in your home or school. What do these things have in common?*

_____

_____

_____

_____

_____

_____

_____

_____

> ▶ **Read**

Underline the object Edison said he could invent.

(Circle) what Edison said he would create to make that invention usable.

The program narrator talks with historian Paul Israel about Edison's most important invention—the light bulb.

Edison Sets a Goal

Narrator: On this historic day—September 15th [1878]—Thomas Edison surprises reporters by announcing his biggest project yet. He says he has solved a problem that has confounded the greatest scientific minds of the nineteenth century—a practical electric lightbulb. As if that were not enough, he says he will also invent a new industry to provide electric power—mysterious invisible energy to run machines and trains. He will harness Niagara Falls to light up America and change the world. [I]ncredibly, he tells the reporters he will have it done in only six weeks....

Edison went to work. He set his Menlo Park team of engineers, mathematicians, glassblowers and draftsmen to the task of creating a practical incandescent lamp.... [They] quickly assembled a number of prototype light bulbs. Not one of them worked.

[Historian] Paul Israel: One of his assistants approached him about all these failed experiments that they had had. He said, "No, they're not failures. They taught [me] something that I didn't know. They taught me what direction to move in...."

Narrator: ...For over a year, [Edison] and his team narrowed down their search for the perfect filament. The breakthrough came in the fourteenth month. The material—a piece of lampblack scraped from the chimney of a common lantern.

confounded: confused or puzzled
harness: make use of
draftsman: person who draws diagrams and plans for an invention
incandescent: producing light by making something hot enough to glow

prototype: an early model
filament: the threadlike wire in a light bulb that electricity flows through, making it glow
lampblack: finely powdered carbon

From: "The American Experience: Edison's Miracle of Light." *PBS Online.* (www.pbs.org/wgbh/amex/edison/filmmore/transcript/index.html)

FIND OUT MORE

SCIENCESAURUS

Current Electricity	317
Electric Circuits	318
Steps in Technology Design	357

SCiLINKS.
THE WORLD'S A CLICK AWAY

www.scilinks.org
Keyword: Light Bulbs
Code: GSPD07

THE FILAMENT SEARCH Some electrical appliances have wires that heat up when the appliance is switched on. A toaster oven and an electric stove are two examples.

▶ *Describe any changes you see in a toaster oven when it is turned on. What other kind of energy besides heat energy is being produced?*

_____

_____

Where there is enough heat, there is light, at least in wires. Edison knew that if he ran an electric current through a wire, the wire would get hot and glow, giving off light.

What makes a wire with current running through it produce heat and light? Resistance. Resistance is a measure of how much a wire resists the movement of electrons through it. The greater the resistance, the greater the amount of heat and light produced.

The amount of resistance in a wire depends on two things: how thick the wire is and how long it is. Thicker wires have less resistance than thinner wires. And shorter wires have less resistance than longer wires.

▶ *Since Edison wanted to produce light, what sort of wire do you think he chose for his light bulb, a thick or thin wire? Explain.*

_____

_____

_____

The light bulb that Edison and his team came up with had a lampblack filament. The lampblack was long and thin and wrapped into a coil shape.

▶ *Why do you suppose Edison's team wrapped the filament into a coil?*

_____

_____

_____

_____

_____

_____

filament

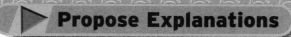

THE MIND OF AN INVENTOR Most inventions are announced to the public after they have been developed and tested. Often the press and other scientists are invited to watch a demonstration of the new product in action.

▶ *How was Edison's announcement about the light bulb different than the usual?*

_____

_____

_____

▶ *What does this tell you about Edison as a person?*

_____

_____

_____

_____

Edison is famous for saying, "Genius is one percent inspiration and 99 percent perspiration."

▶ *How does the reading give clues to what Edison meant?*

_____

_____

_____

_____

Edison said that the unsuccessful light bulbs were not "failures." He learned what would not work and tried something different.

▶ *Describe an experience where you learned from something that might have seemed like a failure.*

_____

_____

_____

_____

65

Edison at Work

Organized Chaos

Edison's research was a group science project that lasted for years.

People often imagine that inventors work all alone in a laboratory. But Edison's approach to inventing was very different.

▲ Edison's laboratory

▶ **Read**

NoteZone

Underline the sentences that describe how Edison worked together with his team.

Circle the sentences that describe how Edison separated himself from his team.

UNIT 2: ELECTRICITY AND MAGNETISM

Later in the transcript, Edison biographer Neil Baldwin talks about Edison's approach to inventing.

A Flitting Butterfly

[Biographer] Neil Baldwin: The second floor of [his research laboratory] was an unobstructed space, like a loft space, you might say. Several people could be working together on one thing, and there were all these notebooks that were next to each project, that were open, that you would write in. You know, whatever you were doing, you would make an entry on that. And Edison was constantly circulating throughout the hall, stopping here and stopping there and working with all the different people all the time, sort of like a butterfly almost, flitting from one flower to another. And then he had his own desk off in the corner by the window, facing the wall. If he sat there, then you weren't supposed to bother him.

I think his hearing loss definitely was one of the reasons why he was able to screen out a lot of buzz from the outside world…. People would say to him, "Why don't you invent a hearing aid? Isn't that an obvious thing for you to want to discover?" He would say, "I want to have this condition, because it helps me be a better creator and a better inventor."

unobstructed: not closed up, open
loft: large open space at the top of a building

circulating: moving around
flitting: moving quickly from place to place

From: "The American Experience: Edison's Miracle of Light." *PBS Online.*
(www.pbs.org/wgbh/amex/edison/filmmore/transcript/index.html)

AN INVENTOR'S WORKSHOP To an outsider, Edison's laboratory might have looked disorganized. It also might have surprised some people to see the boss moving among his workers, rather than working in a separate office.

► *What do you think might be some advantages to Edison's open-space laboratory and his way of supervising his workers?*

_____

_____

_____

_____

_____

Although Edison's laboratory may have looked disorganized, its research methods were not. In science, it is very important to keep careful records of observations and data from experiments. Next to each experiment in Edison's laboratory sat a notebook.

► *Why do you think keeping notebooks by each experiment was better than having each worker carry around his or her own notebook?*

_____

_____

_____

_____

COMPARING SPOKEN AND WRITTEN WORDS The excerpts you have read are from a transcript of the television program, *Edison's Miracle of Light*. A transcript is a written record of everything that was said in a discussion.

► *Read the transcript paragraphs in this lesson carefully. What clues tell you that biographer Neil Baldwin was talking, not reading from a written script? Explain your reasoning.*

_____

_____

_____

_____

_____

Fighting Change

▲ Edison's first electric lighting station

Edison was not just an inventor. He was also a very successful businessman—for a while.

Edison's first electric power generating station, in New York City, was opened in 1882. By the year 1887, there were one hundred and twenty-one Edison central power stations generating electricity in the United States. Each power station was surrounded by the homes and businesses that used the electricity. All the lamps and equipment used in homes and businesses had been made in factories owned by Edison. So it seemed that it would be only a matter of time before Edison would become very wealthy. But when a competitor came along, Edison seemed to lose his confidence.

▶ Before You Read

THINK ABOUT IT Sometimes competition is fun, but sometimes it's scary. People react differently to a challenge. For instance, you might eagerly accept an invitation to play in a tennis match against a well-known older player. Or you might be afraid of looking bad and turn down the invitation, saying that you're too busy to play.

▶ *Think of a time when you, or someone you know, was offered a challenge. Describe that person's reaction. Was the challenge taken as a threat or as an opportunity for friendly competition? Was the challenge accepted or did the person find a reason to avoid the situation? Why do you suppose the person reacted as they did?*

_____

_____

_____

_____

_____

 **Read**

NOTEZONE

Underline ways in which Westinghouse's system differed from Edison's.

Here's what was said in the television show _Edison's Miracle of Light_ about Edison and how he reacted when new competition came on the scene.

Edison vs. Westinghouse

Narrator: ...Edison had shown the world how profitable electric power could be, but now other inventors and other businessmen wanted part of the action. Competitors began rushing into the field with rival products and technological refinements. One of the most threatening of these new competitors was George Westinghouse. Westinghouse challenged Edison with a brand-new system based on high-voltage alternating current. Edison's direct-current power plants could only send electricity a mile or so—any farther away and lightbulbs grew dim—but Westinghouse's newly-developed technology could reach for hundreds of miles with little loss of power. The advantages of alternating current were obvious to most people, but Edison could not or would not see them....

[Biographer] Neil Baldwin: The reason Edison was so against alternating current was not only because it was proposed by a compet[itor], but because, on some level, he saw it as the wave of the future and he saw that ultimately it would win and triumph, and he could see the seeds of his destruction there.

Rather than adapt to the new technology, the inventor who had once been so visionary now decided to fight against change. He launched a new propaganda campaign denouncing alternating current as too dangerous.

---

profitable: making money
competitors: challengers
rival: similar
refinements: improvements
alternating current: electric current that reverses direction back and forth
direct current: electric current that does not reverse direction

ultimately: in the end, eventually
seeds of his destruction: events that would later lead to failure
visionary: full of new ideas
propaganda: one-sided information
campaign: long-term effort to convince
denouncing: criticizing strongly

From: "The American Experience: Edison's Miracle of Light." _PBS Online._
(www.pbs.org/wgbh/amex/edison/filmmore/transcript/index.html)

FIND OUT MORE

SCIENCESAURUS

Current Electricity	317
Electric Circuits	318
Research Bias	368
Tradeoffs	369

COMPARING AC AND DC Electricity is the movement of electrons. Wires are made of metal, and metals have lots of loose electrons. So how do you produce electricity in a wire? You get those electrons to start moving. And how do you do this? With a magnet. All you have to do to produce electricity in a closed loop of wire is to move the wire past a magnet.

If the wire is moved past the magnet in one direction, the electrons will move through the wire in one direction. But if the wire is moved back and forth past the magnet, the electrons will move through the wire in alternating directions.

▶ *Look at the diagrams below. One shows direct current (DC). The other shows alternating current (AC). Based on what you just learned, label each diagram "DC" or "AC." Also indicate which system was used by Edison and which was used by Westinghouse.*

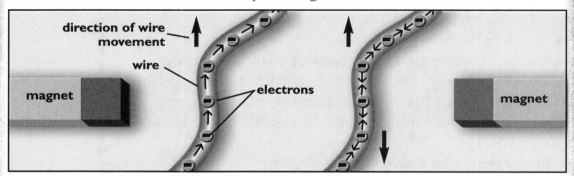

_____   _____

When you send either kind of electricity over very long distances, you always lose some power. Westinghouse and Edison were in agreement on that fact. Both men knew they would have to start out with extremely high voltage electricity at the power plant in order for the electricity to make it out to distant homes and businesses. Voltage is "oomph." With enough voltage, electricity can move long distances over wires. But high voltage is also extremely dangerous. If you sent it into people's houses you could kill them!

What Westinghouse knew that Edison didn't was how to build a little device called a transformer. A transformer can raise or lower the voltage of AC electricity.

▶ *How could Westinghouse use a transformer to keep people safe in their homes but still send out high-voltage electricity from the power plant?*

_____

_____

_____

_____

UNDERSTANDING EDISON Edison was an inventor. But he was also a business owner. Banks had given him money to build his electrical power companies. It took a long time for him to make his companies profitable.

▶ *Why do you think Edison the business person was against AC electricity?*

_____

_____

_____

_____

Actually, Edison didn't completely understand AC electricity. He had taught himself most of what he knew about science. He didn't have all the necessary math skills to understand AC electricity.

▶ *How might Edison's education have affected his response to AC electricity?*

_____

_____

_____

_____

 ▶ **Take Action**

WHERE DOES YOUR POWER COME FROM? To create electricity, either a wire is moved past a magnet, or a magnet is moved past a wire. That movement takes energy. So, in order to generate electricity, power plants first need some other source of energy. Some burn a fuel such as oil for energy. Others get their energy from nuclear reactions, and some get energy from the power of waterfalls.

People disagree about what the best source of energy for generating electricity is. Do research to find out what sources of energy are used in power plants in your area. Then find out the pros and cons of using that type of energy. Decide whether you think this is the best possible source of energy for your area, or whether you think another source would be better.

▶ *Make a poster to show your position. Make your poster persuasive by showing important facts and using interesting graphics.*

MAKE A POSTER

It's Magnetic

TONGUES OF FLAME

What's that up in the sky?

Nineteenth-century polar explorers had to be hardy and courageous. They saw their adventure as a test of their character. They also hoped to become rich and famous. But when they saw the northern lights—also called the aurora borealis—they became poets. The aurora is a spectacular light show that occurs in the skies mainly near Earth's north and south poles. In 1893, the crew of the Norwegian ship *Fram* was treated to one such light show as they were trapped in the arctic ice around the north pole.

▲ **Aurora borealis**

NoteZone

Underline the action verbs that describe the aurora.

 Read

Fram sailor Fridtjof Nansen was so moved by seeing the northern lights that he wrote about it in his journal.

Aurora in the Sky

Presently the aurora borealis shakes over the vault of heaven its veil of glittering silver—changing now to green, now to red. It spreads, it contracts again, in restless change, next it breaks into waving, many-folded bands of shining silver, over which shoots billows of glittering rays; and then the glory vanishes. Presently it shimmers in tongues of flame over the very zenith; and then again it shoots a bright ray right up from the horizon, until the whole melts away in the moonlight, and it is as though one heard the sigh of a departing spirit. Here and there are left a few waving streamers of light, vague as a foreboding—they are the dust from the aurora's glittering cloak.

vault: arch that forms a ceiling
billows: big waves
zenith: the highest point
horizon: where the sky seems to meet earth or sea

vague: dim or unclear
foreboding: a feeling that something bad will happen
cloak: long, loose coat

FIND OUT MORE

SCIENCESAURUS

Electricity and
Magnetism   314
Magnetism   320

SCiLINKS
THE WORLD'S A CLICK AWAY

www.scilinks.org
Keyword: Earth's
Magnetic Field
Code: GSPD08

From Savage, Candace. *Aurora: The Mysterious Northern Lights*. Sierra Club Books.

UNIT 2: ELECTRICITY AND MAGNETISM

▶ **Explore**

WHAT CAUSES AN AURORA? What do you think of when you hear the word *magnet*? You might picture a horseshoe magnet or the bar magnet on a toy. You probably don't, however, think about Earth. But Earth too acts as a sort of giant magnet.

Like any magnet, Earth has a north and south pole. It also has a magnetic field that surrounds it. This magnetic field acts like a shield, protecting Earth from charged particles that come towards it from the sun.

Look at the diagram below. It shows the magnetic lines of force that describe the shape of the magnetic field around Earth.

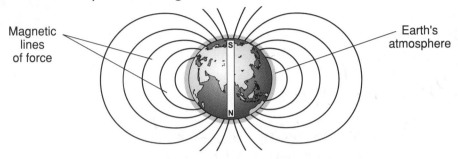

Magnetic lines of force

Earth's atmosphere

▶ *What do you notice about the lines of force near the poles? How are they different from the lines of force near other parts of Earth?*

_____

_____

▶ *Imagine charged particles coming in from the sun toward Earth. Where do you think the particles would be most likely to enter Earth's atmosphere?*

_____

_____

Auroras form where charged particles from the sun enter Earth's atmosphere.

▶ *Look at a map of Earth. Why do you think auroras are more likely to be seen in Alaska and New Zealand than in Mexico and Texas?*

_____

_____

_____

_____

It's Magnetic

Coming Home

How would you find your way home if you were in the middle of the ocean?

The migration route of a loggerhead turtle is more than 12,000 kilometers long and takes anywhere from 5–10 years to complete. Turtles can't read maps, so how do they find their way along this amazing journey? Scientists have found that these turtles have their own built-in navigation system based on magnetism. This system lets them know at any time exactly where they are on Earth, and what direction they are heading!

▲ A loggerhead turtle

Before You Read

FINDING YOUR WAY People use different tools and clues to help them find their way when they travel. Maps show us where we are, and the streets or paths we need to take to get somewhere else. Or maybe we already know where we are going, but we use certain objects as clues to know when and where to make the correct turns to get us there.

► *Think about the route you take to school each morning. Maybe you walk, or maybe you are driven. What clues from the environment (objects) do you use that tell you the correct route to take?*

_____

_____

_____

_____

A compass is a tool that uses Earth's magnetic field to tell you which direction you should go in order to head north, south, east, or west.

► *Describe a situation where having a compass might be helpful to you.*

_____

_____

_____

_____

UNIT 2: ELECTRICITY AND MAGNETISM

▶ Read

NOTEZONE

Underline how Earth's magnetic field influences a traveling sea turtle.

Kathy Wollard, who writes for the newspaper *Newsday*, answers science questions from young readers. Here she answers a question about the wandering ways of sea turtles.

Magnetic Personalities

"How can sea turtles find their way back to the place where they were born after many years to lay eggs?" asks Ving Kim of Flushing, [New York].

Scientists think sea turtles navigate the oceans by sensing Earth's magnetic fields and following them like a map.

Arcing out from the north and south ends of our planet is an invisible magnetic force field... Overall, Earth's magnetic field is only approximately 1/20,000th as strong as that of a refrigerator magnet, so it can't attract paper clips. But it can influence a swinging compass needle—or a traveling sea turtle.

In experiments with newborn sea turtles, when scientists changed the direction of a magnetic field in a saltwater tank, swimming turtles would change direction, too. Baby sea turtles apparently sense both the direction and intensity of the Earth's field. Regional magnetic fields are like navigational buoys to turtles in the open sea, helping them to stay on course and swim in the warmest, food-rich currents.

navigate: steer a course
arcing: following a curved line
intensity: strength
regional: in a small area

buoys: floating objects that mark a spot
currents: moving rivers of ocean water

From: Wollard, Kathy. "Sea Turtles' Magnetic Personalities." *Newsday.*

FIND OUT MORE

SCIENCESAURUS

Electricity and	
Magnetism	314
Magnetism	320
Electromagnetism	321

SCILINKS.
THE WORLD'S A CLICK AWAY

www.scilinks.org
Keyword: Earth's
Magnetic Field
Code: GSPD08

FOLLOW THAT TURTLE The path on the map below shows the approximate migration route of loggerhead turtles in the North Atlantic Ocean. Ocean currents are shown as black arrows.

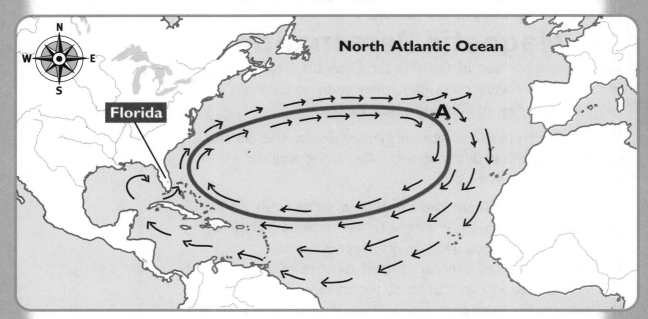

The turtles hatch on the beaches of eastern Florida. Soon they head east and enter the ocean currents that will take them around the Atlantic. The turtles use the ocean currents to help carry them on their journey, but scientists think they use Earth's magnetic field to help them stay on the correct course.

Earth acts like a giant, weak magnet. Like any magnet, Earth has a north pole and a south pole. The magnetic field is strongest at these places. It gets weaker as you move towards the equator. At the equator, the field is the weakest.

Researchers hypothesize that loggerhead turtles can detect Earth's magnetic field—both the direction (north or south) and the strength (strong or weak).

▶ *Look at point "A" on the map. What is happening to the ocean currents at this place?*

_____

▶ *How might a loggerhead turtle use the strength of Earth's magnetic field to know if it went the wrong way at point "A"?*

_____

_____

_____

_____

▶ Propose Explanations

WHICH WAY IS UP? The group of researchers wanted to test their hypothesis that loggerhead turtles are able to use Earth's magnetic field to determine direction (north or south). So they set up an experiment.

The researchers put a number of baby turtles in a big pool in the laboratory. They then created a magnetic field around the pool by wrapping large coils of wire around it and running electricity through the wire. (Electricity running through a wire creates a magnetic field around the wire.) This magnetic field was meant to imitate Earth's magnetic field. By changing the direction the electricity traveled through the wire, they could change the direction of the magnetic field around the pool.

The researchers found that when they changed the direction the electricity flowed through the wire, the turtles in the pool started swimming in the opposite direction.

▶ *How does this result support the researchers' hypothesis?*

_____

_____

_____

_____

▶ Take Action

RESEARCH OTHER MAGNETIC PERSONALITIES Sea turtles are not the only animals that use magnetism to navigate. Honeybees, monarch butterflies, green sea turtles, a bird called the bobolink, a salamander called the eastern red-spotted newt, frogs, homing pigeons, trout, sharks, and whales do, too. How do they do it?

Choose an animal with a magnetic personality. Go to the library or use the Internet to find out how the animal uses magnetism and how scientists think it works. Be sure to include how far the animal migrates and where it lives during different times of the year.

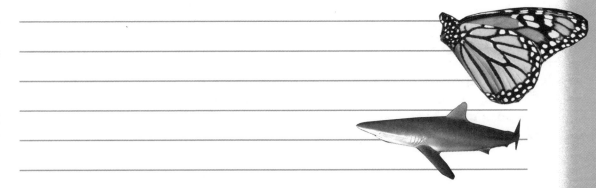

_____

_____

_____

_____

_____

It's Magnetic

On the Fast Track

How would you like to ride a train that would move you to your destination almost as fast as a plane?

Imagine getting in a bullet-shaped train and gliding to your destination at almost 500 kilometers (about 300 miles) per hour. Magnetism could make it possible. In the early 1960s, two American scientists patented a new kind of train called a *maglev* train. The name stands for "magnetically levitated train," because the train floats just above the track. Maglev trains are very expensive to build, but several different groups are experimenting with new designs that could slash the costs greatly. If these designs prove practical, we could someday see maglev trains zooming between American cities.

▶ **Before You Read**

ZOOM! Maglev trains use magnets to float a fraction of an inch above the tracks. To get an idea how this works, experiment with two bar magnets.

Look at the magnets. One end should be marked "S" (south) and one end marked "N" (north). Place both north poles together, then both south poles together, and finally, one north pole and one south pole together.

▶ *In the space below, draw pictures to show what you did and what you observed.*

▶ *What conclusion can you draw about how magnets behave? Use the following terms:* like poles, opposite poles, attract, *and* repel *(push away).*

_____

_____

> **Read**

Chana Steifel calls us "all aboard" in this article from *Science World*.

FAST TRACK

All aboard the "Maglev Express"—the world's fastest train, propelled through the air by magnets!

How does maglev work? The process is repulsive. No, it won't turn your stomach. Repulsion is a property of magnetism. In the case of the maglev train, electromagnets (coils of wire magnetized by electric currents) on the bottom of the train repel, or push against, other electromagnets in the guideway tracks. That causes the train to float....

To propel the train forward, an alternating current of electricity flows through coils in the guideway walls. The current causes each coil to change its polarity (N to S; S to N) as each train magnet passes. When the train and guideway magnets line up N-N or S-S, the result is repulsion, or a "push" forward. All that pushing and pulling makes maglevs fly.

To make the train speed up or slow down, engineers controlling the railway increase or decrease the amount of electric power fed into the track. That changes the speed at which the magnetic wave travels underneath the train.

propelled: moved or pushed
repulsive: pushing away
guideway: a channel that controls the direction the maglev train moves in
alternating current: current that travels in one direction and then another

polarity: direction

From: Stiefel, Chana. "Fast Track." *Science World*.

NOTEZONE

Underline what causes the train to float.

Circle what engineers do to change the speed of the train.

FIND OUT MORE

SCIENCESAURUS

Electricity and
  Magnetism   314
Magnetism   320
Electromagnetism 321

▼ A maglev train in Japan

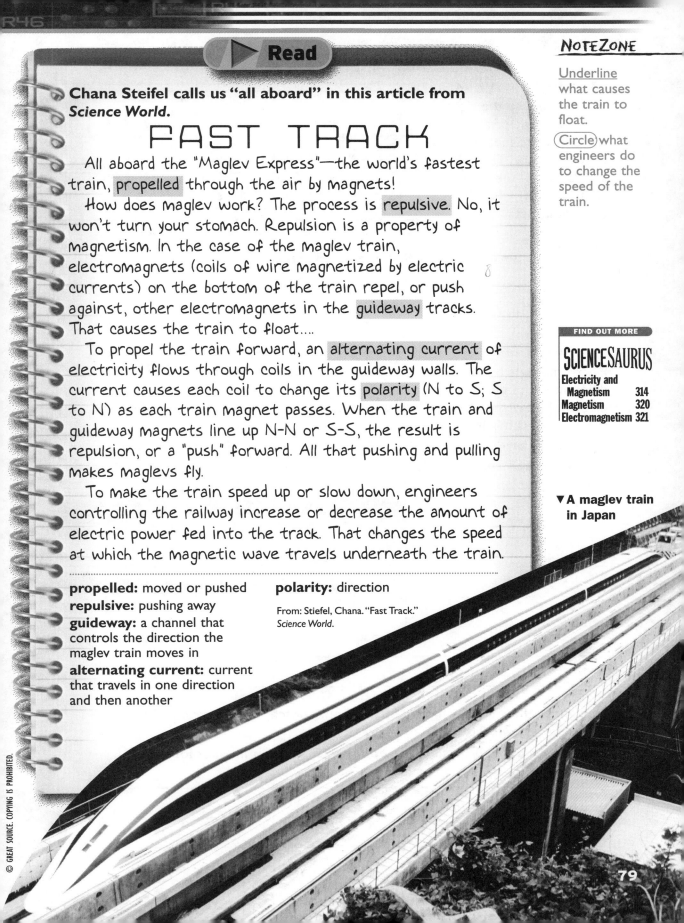

Explore

PUSH ME, PULL ME

The diagram to the right shows a maglev train and the electromagnets that lift it off the track. The "N" and "S" show the north or south polarity of each electromagnet.

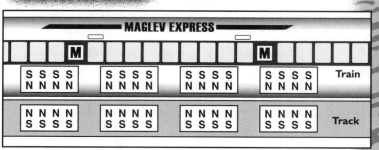

▲ Side view of maglev train floating above track

▶ *Study the diagram. What allows the train to float above the track?*

_____

_____

_____

Electromagnets below a maglev train lift it off the track. A completely different set of electromagnets beside the train make it move forward. The diagram below shows how electromagnets on the sides of the train and on the guideways might be arranged.

▶ *Draw an arrow to show which direction you think this train is moving.*

▶ *Why do you think the train is moving that direction?*

_____

_____

_____

_____

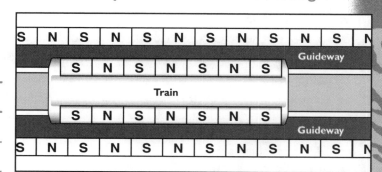

▲ Top view of maglev train moving between guideways

As soon as the train has moved forward one "notch," the electromagnets on the guideways will flip to the opposite polarity.

▶ *Explain how you think that could keep the train moving forward.*

_____

_____

_____

80

YOUR OWN MAGNET TRAIN

Build an electromagnet to power a train of paper clips.

What You Need:

- 6-volt dry cell
- scissors or wire stripper
- long steel nail
- paper clips
- plastic-covered copper wire (1 m)
- 4 drinking glasses
- square piece of cardboard
- tape

What to Do:

1. First, make an electromagnet. Strip the insulation off about 5 cm at the ends of the wire.
2. Wrap the wire at least 12 times around the nail. (The more you wrap it, the more powerful your electromagnet will be.)
3. Connect the ends of the wires to the posts of the dry cell.
4. Pass the nail over a pile of paper clips. The nail should attract the clips. Disconnect one wire and the clips will fall.
5. Now set up your train. Draw your train track on the cardboard. Tape each corner of the cardboard to a drinking glass.
6. Hook the paper clips into a train and put them on the track.
7. Move the electromagnet below the cardboard to pull your train around the track.

What Do You See?

▶ *What force moved your train along the track?*

_____

_____

▶ *How is your model train similar to a maglev train? How is it different?*

_____

_____

_____

_____

Plowboy Inventor

How did a field of sugar beets inspire a 14-year-old boy to help invent something that would change the world?

Inventors get their ideas by looking at the world around them. Does the shape of an airplane remind you of anything? Maybe a bird? Early flight engineers looked at birds when coming up with ideas about how to build a machine that could fly. Even the neatly plowed rows of a sugar-beet field could be inspiring to a young electronics engineer.

Electronics is a type of technology that deals with electrons in motion. You use electronics every time you watch TV, talk on the phone, or use the computer.

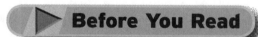
Before You Read

USING ELECTRONICS

▶ *How do you personally use electronics in your daily life? Describe what you use and how it helps you.*

_____

_____

_____

_____

_____

_____

_____

_____

UNIT 2: ELECTRICITY AND MAGNETISM

▶ Read

NOTEZONE

Underline the image in nature that inspired Philo's invention.

Philo T. Farnsworth spent his boyhood days working on the family farm in Rigby, Idaho. Plowing the sugar-beet fields one day in 1921, he was suddenly hit by an idea that led him to invent television.

Imagine That!

Philo was an avid reader of popular-science magazines. Inspired by articles in their pages, he had been trying for more than a year to figure out how to create television. As his future wife later wrote, "Bit by bit he collected information that eventually led him to discover for himself that mysterious, vitally important particle called the electron, the study of which would define his life.... Philo tried to imagine a way to use electrons to eliminate the mechanical method of transmitting pictures." The solution first came to him when he looked back over his shoulder in the sugar-beet field. He saw the neat rows his harrow had just made in the earth. The pattern gave him an idea for using electrons in similar rows to make the television picture.

FIND OUT MORE

SCIENCESAURUS

Atomic Structure	256
Current Electricity	317
Electric Circuits	318
Magnetism	320
Electromagnetism	321

avid: very eager
vitally: extremely
eliminate: get rid of
mechanical: using a machine with moving parts
transmitting: sending
harrow: plow

From: Tucker, Tom. *Brainstorm! The Stories of Twenty American Kid Inventors.* Farrar, Straus and Giroux.

An early television set ▶

SENDING AN IMAGE A television camera's job is to take an image from one place and send it to another place—your television. The question is, how can the image be sent?

Think about a 1000-piece jigsaw puzzle. The image it shows is made up of 1000 smaller pieces of the image. Let's say you had a completed jigsaw puzzle. And let's say you wanted to pass the puzzle to a friend in the next room, but there was a wall between you with only a small hole in it.

▶ *How might you transfer the puzzle to your friend?*

_____

_____

▶ *How could you make it very easy for your friend to reassemble the puzzle? Record your ideas.*

_____

_____

_____

Now think about a television camera. It takes an image, breaks it down into many tiny parts, and sends the parts to your television. Your television then puts the parts back together to re-form the image. Each "part" is an electric signal (electrons) sent through a wire.

This drawing of a television camera is one that Philo made while he was still in high school. The picture shows the lens of the camera on the left. The lens focuses the optical (light) image onto a photoelectric plate. This plate changes the light into electrical signals that form an electron image. The signals then travel through wires to your television. Strong light produces strong signals, while low light produces weaker signals. In this way, the signals can carry information about light and dark areas of the image.

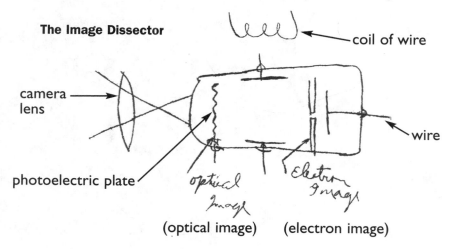

The Image Dissector

coil of wire

camera lens

wire

photoelectric plate

(optical image)   (electron image)

Philo called his camera the Image Dissector. To *dissect* something means to take it apart.

▶ *Why do you think Philo called his camera the Image Dissector?*

_____

_____

Philo came up with the idea of using a magnetic field to hold the electrons in straight rows as they came off of the photoelectric plate and moved toward the wires. Philo knew that electric current moving through a wire creates a magnetic field. So he wrapped the Dissector with a coil of wire carrying an electric current. This produced a magnetic field around the Dissector that guided the electrons in rows as orderly as those he saw in his beet field.

▶ *Why do you think it was important that the electrons traveled in an orderly way? (Hint: Think about passing the jigsaw puzzle pieces to your friend in the next room.)*

_____

_____

SIGNALS CREATE AN IMAGE Look at the following series of "electric signals." Imagine that they are coming through the wire to your black-and-white television. An "off" signal produces a tiny black square on the screen. An "on" signal produces a tiny white square. When you stand back, all the tiny squares work together to form a larger image.

off–off–off–off–off–off–on–on–on–off–off–on–off–on–off–off–on–on–
on–off–off–on–off–off–off–off–on–off–off–off–off–on–off–off–off

▶ *Fill in the "screen" below to see the image formed by the electric signals received. Begin at the top left. If the signal is "on," leave the box blank. If the signal is "off," blacken the box with your pencil.*

1	2	3	4	5
6	7	8	9	10
11	12	13	14	15
16	17	18	19	20
21	22	23	24	25
26	27	28	29	30
31	32	33	34	35

▶ *What do you see on your "screen"?*

_____

Electronics

▼ Telephone wires

A Copper Wire

Copper wires have made it possible for us to talk with people around the world whenever we want.

Have you ever wondered how your voice is carried from your home telephone to the telephone of a friend many miles away? Here's a hint: Look at the wires that connect your phone to the wall, and the wires that run from one telephone pole to another. Your words travel as electric signals through these wires, connecting you to people all over the country.

▶ **Read**

NOTEZONE

In line 4, Sandburg lists examples of something he calls "it." What is the "it"?

FIND OUT MORE

SCIENCESAURUS

Current Electricity   317
Electric Circuits   318

SCILINKS
THE WORLD'S A CLICK AWAY

www.scilinks.org
Keyword: Alexander Graham Bell
Code: GSPD09

Carl Sandburg (1878–1967) was one of America's greatest poets. In 1916 he wrote a poem praising the thin copper wires that connected Americans.

Under a Telephone Pole

I AM a copper wire slung in the air,

Slim against the sun I make not even a clear line of shadow.

Night and day I keep singing—humming and thrumming:

It is love and war and money; it is the fighting and the tears, the work and want,

Death and laughter of men and women passing through me, carrier of your speech,

In the rain and the wet dripping, in the dawn and the shine drying,

A copper wire.

From: Sandburg, Carl. *Chicago Poems.*

Explore

HOW A TELEPHONE WORKS Put your fingers on your throat and say the alphabet out loud.

► *What do you feel?* _____

When you speak, vibrations in your voice box create sound waves that travel through the air to the ear of someone nearby. But sound waves can't travel through telephone wires.

Look at the following diagram of a telephone. When you talk into the mouthpiece (the transmitter), your voice vibrates a metal disk. These vibrations are then converted to an electric current that varies just as your voice varies as you speak. This varying current moves through telephone wires to the phone of your friend. There, in the earpiece (receiver), the electric current is converted back to sound waves and your friend hears your voice.

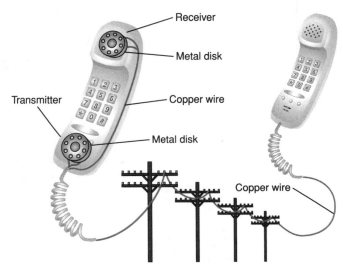

► *In the space below, draw a graphic organizer that shows the energy conversions involved in a telephone call.*

► *What form of energy is the copper wire described in the poem carrying?*

_____

Electronics

Zeroes and Ones

In the 1800s, a woman created the code of computer technology.

Ada Byron Lovelace lived during a time when women did not study mathematics. Back in the 1800s, few girls even went to school. But Ada's father was a famous poet. Her mother was a mathematician and a member of the royal family in England. This meant she had opportunities other women did not, including a private tutor. Ada's tutor introduced her to other mathematicians. These meetings led Ada to make a suggestion that would change the world.

Her suggestion had to do with the binary number system, which uses only the digits 0 and 1 instead of all the digits from 0 to 9. Today, all computers use the binary number system to store and transmit information.

▲ Ada Byron Lovelace

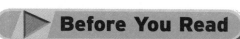 **Before You Read**

BREAKING THE CODE Codes are invented for many purposes. Sometimes a code is used to send secret messages. The person who receives the coded message has a "key" to unlock the code. See if you can translate this coded message using the key provided.

Nbui dbo cf gvo.

(key: a ⟶ b)

► *What was the secret to this code?*

_____

_____

_____

▶ **Read**

NOTEZONE

What more do you want to know after reading this?

Ada's private tutor introduced her to mathematician and inventor Charles Babbage. At the time, Babbage was working on a calculating machine he called the *difference engine.*

ANALYTICAL ENGINE

Soon after that, Ada and her mother were invited to Babbage's workshop, where he described his project. He was building a machine that would be capable of calculating tables of numbers by computing their differences. At that time, all [complex calculations were done] by hand, which was extremely time consuming, and filled with errors. When Ada saw the machine, she immediately recognized its tremendous potential. She began to work with Babbage....

▼ **Babbage's analytical engine**

After many years of working on the difference engine, [Babbage] abandoned it for a better plan—the analytical engine. This machine would be able to do much more than generate tables. It would perform a variety of functions by receiving commands from a series of punched cards. Babbage got this idea from a weaving loom designed by J. M. Jacquard. If the cards could tell the loom which threads to pick up, Babbage reasoned they could direct the machine as to which gears to operate.

computing: calculating
analytical: something that breaks down and examines data in order to understand it
generate: make
functions: tasks

weaving loom: a machine that weaves threads together to create cloth
gears: toothed wheels that make up the mechanical part of the analytical engine
operate: make work

FIND OUT MORE

SCIENCESAURUS
Science, Technology and Society 354
Decimals 378

www.scilinks.org
Keyword: Computer Technology
Code: GSPD10

From: Reimer, Luetta and Wilbert Reimer. *Mathematicians Are People, Too. Stories from the Lives of Great Mathematicians Vol 2.* Pearson Education, Inc., publishing as Dale Seymour Publications.

BINARY NUMBERS The decimal number system we use everyday is a "base 10" system that uses ten digits—0, 1, 2, 3, 4, 5, 6, 7, 8, and 9. Computers, on the other hand, can only read two digits—0 and 1. That's because computers are electronic devices and can only read whether a switch is ON or OFF. To a machine, the digit 1 means ON, and 0 means OFF. The two-digit number system computers use is called the "base 2" system, or binary number system.

Use the table below to help you translate the decimal numbers 12, 13, and 20 into binary numbers. First, finish filling in the binary place values in the second row of the chart. (The first three have been done for you.) The small number above the "2" tells you how many times to multiply the "2" by itself. So, for example, 2^2 becomes 2 x 2 or 4. Similarly, 2^3 becomes 2 x 2 x 2.

BINARY PLACE VALUES							
2^7	2^6	2^5	2^4	2^3	2^2	2^1	2^0
					4	2	1
12							
13							
20							

Now, follow these steps to convert the number 12, in the third row, to binary:
1. Find the greatest place value that is less than or equal to 12. This is 8, so write a "1" in the eights place to show that you have one group of 8.
2. Then, since you need 4 more to make 12, write a "1" in the fours place.
3. Fill in the empty boxes to the right of the 1s with 0s as placeholders.
▶ *What is the sequence of 1s and 0s in base 2 that has the same value as 12 in base 10?*

Now try converting 13.
1. Begin by writing a "1" in the eights place to show that 13 has one group of 8.
2. You need 5 more to make 13. Put "1"s in the two places that add up to 5.
3. Fill in the empty boxes between the 1s with 0s as placeholders.
▶ *What is the sequence of 1s and 0s in base 2 that has the same value as 13 in base 10?*

Go to the last row of the chart and fill in the boxes to show the binary form of the number 20.
▶ *What is the sequence of 1s and 0s that has the value of 20 in base 10?*

HOW IS BINARY CODE USED IN COMPUTERS? What does the computer do with this binary code? A "1" turns a switch controlling electric current ON. A "0" turns a switch controlling electric current OFF. As the flow of electric current is started and stopped, operations like calculating and writing letters are performed.

For example, when you send e-mail to a friend, you use words and letters. But the computer "codes" each letter into a number. Almost all computers use a standard code called ASCII. In ASCII code, all letters are coded as base 10 numbers. Then the computer changes these numbers into binary code. But that is not all it has to do.

The computer must read numbers as bytes. A byte is a group of eight binary digits made of 1s and 0s. It changes each binary number into an eight-digit number by adding 0s onto the beginning. For example, the number 1 would be 00000001. To write numbers the way a computer reads them, use exactly eight digits (0 or 1) each time you write a number.

▶ *Go back to the chart on page 90. Fill in the chart with 0s as needed to make each number a byte.*

▶ *What byte represents the base 10 number "12" in binary code?*

_____

Take Action

WRITE A MESSAGE IN COMPUTER CODE The table below shows the base 10 ASCII code for all lower case letters. Write the word "hi" in ASCII code. Then convert each ASCII code number in the word into an eight-digit binary number (byte). Use the chart on page 90 to help you with the conversion.

ASCII code for lower case letters							
a	97	h	104	o	111	v	118
b	98	i	105	p	112	w	119
c	99	j	106	q	113	x	120
d	100	k	107	r	114	y	121
e	101	l	108	s	115	z	122
f	102	m	109	t	116		
g	103	n	110	u	117		

ASCII _____

Binary _____

Sound, Light, and Heat

Switch on the radio, flip on the light, and sit by the fire.
Sound, light, and heat may seem very different, but all have something in common. They are all forms of energy. Sound we can hear, light we can see, and heat we can feel. These forms of energy can also cause objects around them to change. We don't think of sound as breaking objects very often. But like all forms of energy, sound is capable of changing matter.

In this lesson you will look at different forms of energy—how they travel and what effect they have on objects around them. You'll find out how astronauts protect themselves from getting sunburned in space and how doctors can use sound to help heal patients. You'll see how mirrors can be used to create optical illusions and why certain fabrics keep you warmer than others.

? Did You Know?

Astronauts in space have to touch their helmets together in order to hear each other talk. That's because sound waves need to travel through a medium, and there is no air in space. But the sound waves can travel through the solid materials that make up the helmet.

The Energy of Waves

Battering Waves

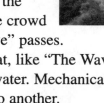

Would you want to battle stormy ocean waves in a small sailboat?

Have you ever seen "The Wave" in a sports stadium? The fans in one area stand up and raise their hands in the air. As they begin to lower their arms and sit back down, the people beside them stand up and raise their arms. Then they sit and lower their arms, and so on. Fans on the other side of the stadium see a "wave" moving across the stadium. The crowd is the medium, or substance, through which this "wave" passes.

Water waves are mechanical waves. This means that, like "The Wave," they can only travel through matter. In this case the matter is water. Mechanical waves, including water waves, carry energy from one place to another.

▶ **Before You Read**

WATER WAVES Think about times when you have seen waves. You might have seen them in an ocean, lake, pond, or pool. Perhaps you've seen a movie or television show where a boat was being knocked about by the waves. Or, maybe you've even had such an experience of your own.

▶ *What experiences have you had with waves? Describe one experience.*

_____

_____

_____

_____

_____

_____

_____

_____

_____

_____

▶ **Read**

In the novel *The Voyage of the Frog*, a 14-year-old boy named David sails alone into the Pacific Ocean aboard the *Frog*, a small sailboat. During a storm, the waves threaten his boat and his life.

The Voyage of the Frog

The wind had increased in strength. He climbed onto the cabin and reefed the main [sail] down to half size but left the jib full. Then he went back to the helm, brought her around, and the sails filled and the *Frog* started taking the swells.

There were waves coming in now as well, on top of the swells, growing in chop and intensity each moment. The *Frog* was slamming, making noise, but he held her angled up into the wind and took it. Spray came over the bow and covered him, soaking him, but he...would not...let the sea have her....

The wind became worse. The waves grew until they were larger than the swells they rode on, towering over him, burying the bow. More than once he was knocked off his feet by a wall of water coming back over the side of the cabin but he never let go of the helm, rose and took it again and again, held her through wave after wave when they rose over him, walls of water, mountains of water moving down on him, down on the *Frog*.

Underline three clues to the amount of energy in the waves.

FIND OUT MORE

SCIENCESAURUS

Characteristics of a Wave	306
Kinds of Waves	307

SCI LINKS
THE WORLD'S A CLICK AWAY

www.scilinks.org
Keyword: Ocean Waves
Code: GSPD11

---

reefed: reduced the size of the sail by rolling it and tying it down
jib: a triangular sail in front of the main sail
helm: the steering wheel of a boat

swells: long waves that move continuously without breaking
chop: short, slapping motion
intensity: strength
bow: front section of a boat

From: Paulsen, Gary. *The Voyage of the Frog.* Orchard Books.

WIND AND WAVES Sailors—like David in *The Voyage of the Frog*—depend on energy from the wind to power their boats. Moving air particles push against the sails and move the boat forward.

Winds blowing over the ocean also transfer their energy to the water, creating ocean waves. The size of the waves created by wind and the amount of energy they contain is determined by several factors. Three of these factors are shown in the chart. Each one affects the amount of energy that is transferred from the wind to the water. The greater the amount of energy that is transferred, the larger the waves are.

Factors Affecting the Size of Water Waves		
Wind Velocity	**Wind Duration**	**Fetch**
the speed at which the wind blows in a certain direction	the length of time the wind blows	the area the wind blows over

▶ *What can you infer about the velocity of the wind in the reading from* **The Voyage of the Frog?** *What clues help you make this inference?*

_____

_____

_____

▶ *What can you infer about the duration of the wind in the reading? What clues help you make this inference?*

_____

_____

_____

▶ *What can you infer about the fetch of the wind? What clues help you make this inference?*

_____

_____

_____

▶ *What do the clues about wind velocity, wind duration, and fetch tell you about the amount of energy in the waves that struck the Frog?*

_____

_____

HOW STRONG ARE THE WAVES? All water waves have the same basic shape. The dashed line in the diagram represents the water surface at rest. A wave moving along the water surface has a crest and a trough. The crest is the highest point of the wave and the trough is the lowest. Amplitude is the distance from the resting point to the crest of the wave. The greater the amplitude, the greater the amount of energy the wave carries.

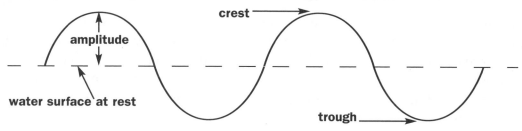

▶ *What can you infer about the amplitude of the waves that struck the Frog? What evidence do you have?*

_____

_____

▶ *What does this tell you about the amount of energy in the waves in the story?*

_____

_____

▶ *The wind transferred some of its energy to the water, making waves. What did the waves transfer some of their energy to? What evidence do you have?*

_____

_____

▶ **Take Action**

THAT'S DISTURBING! In *The Voyage of the Frog*, the wind's motion is the "disturbing force" that creates the ocean waves. Every mechanical wave has a disturbing force that creates it. For each kind of wave below, write what might be the disturbing force. If necessary, do some research to get ideas.

Mechanical Wave	Disturbing Force
A flag waving at the top of a flagpole	
Ripples in a pond	
Vibrations of a guitar string	

97

The Energy of Waves

Do Astronauts Get SUNBURNED?

With no protection, an astronaut in space would be sunburned in just seconds.

Imagine standing on a beach watching the waves come in to shore. Step into the water and you can feel each wave hit your legs. While you stand there, other waves are hitting you, too. They are waves that come from the sun and they are called electromagnetic waves. Like all waves, electromagnetic waves carry energy. While water waves can only travel through matter, electromagnetic waves can also travel through a vacuum, or a place without matter. Much of space is a vacuum.

When astronauts go into space, they must wear space suits, complete with gloves and helmets, to survive in the vacuum. Inside their space suits they have oxygen to breathe. Space suits also protect them from the energy of the sun's electromagnetic waves.

▶ **Before You Read**

FEEL THE BURN Have you ever been sunburned? Where were you? Do you remember what the weather was like? What time of year was it? What time of day? Do you remember what you were wearing? Write about your experience.

_____

_____

_____

_____

_____

_____

_____

_____

_____

UNIT 3: SOUND, LIGHT, AND HEAT

NOTEZONE

Underline the type of electro-magnetic waves that can give you a sunburn.

Circle what protects you from electro-magnetic waves when you are on Earth.

What would happen if an astronaut took off a glove during a space walk? Here's how physics professor Philip Plait answered that question.

WHAT DOES OUTER SPACE FEEL LIKE?

Space doesn't feel like anything, because there is nothing to feel! Space is a vacuum (or near enough). It's a common question to ask how hot space is (or how cold), but space itself has no temperature. However, the Sun is hot, and [it gives off that energy in the form of electromagnetic waves]. You [or any other object] absorb [some of] that [energy] and feel heat. Near the Earth, a person floating in space would...not receive enough [heat energy] to keep from freezing! You yourself would radiate away your heat, and that's why spacesuits have heaters in them....

Surprisingly, the worst thing that might happen [if you took off your glove] is that you'd get a bad sunburn. Without the Earth's protective ozone layer between you and the raw sunlight, the ultraviolet light from the Sun could give you a nasty sunburn in just a few seconds! If you're an astronaut doing a tricky maneuver, better pack the sunblock!

ozone layer: a layer of the atmosphere
ultraviolet light: high-energy electromagnetic waves
maneuver: a procedure requiring skill

From: Guess, Malcolm. "What Does Outer Space Feel Like?" *Bad Astronomy.* (www.badastronomy.com/mad/1999/space_feel.html)

FIND OUT MORE

SCIENCESAURUS

Characteristics of a Wave	306
Kinds of Waves	307
Electromagnetic Spectrum	309

Astronaut Winston Scott ▶ in a spacesuit, on Columbia mission STS-87

INTERPRET A DIAGRAM The diagram shows all the types of electromagnetic waves given off by the sun. The waves are in the order of their frequencies, starting with the lower frequencies at the left. Remember, frequency is the measure of how many waves pass by a point each second.

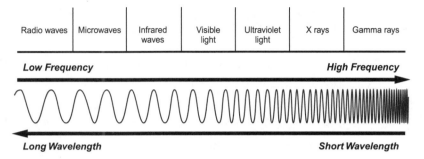

The higher the frequency of the waves, the more energy they carry. The more energy a wave carries, the more dangerous it is to living things. Luckily, the atmosphere protects Earth from most high-energy waves. You read that a layer of ozone in the atmosphere protects us from most of the ultraviolet light from the sun. But some ultraviolet light still gets through.

► *Why might ultraviolet light waves cause sunburn when visible light waves do not?*

_____

_____

WHICH WAVES ARE SAFE? All the electromagnetic waves shown in the diagram above are given off by sources other than the sun as well. Radios and microwave ovens are common household objects. Infrared heat lamps are used in restaurants to keep food warm. Every room at home has at least one light bulb that gives off visible light. Ultraviolet lamps are sometimes used at amusement parks to give a Day-Glo effect. Other types of electromagnetic waves are used only by trained professionals. X rays are used by doctors to create pictures of the body. Gamma rays are used in hospitals to sterilize medical equipment.

► *Mark each type of electromagnetic wave shown on the diagram above. Use an "E" to label the types that can be used by everyone. Use an "S" to label the types that require special training.*

► *How are the frequencies of the waves related to who can use them? Why do you think this is?*

_____

_____

_____

ULTRAVIOLET WAVES AND SKIN Scientists have discovered a direct connection between exposure to ultraviolet light and certain kinds of skin damage. Scientists don't know exactly how ultraviolet light damages skin. What they do know is that the energy of these waves causes chemical reactions inside skin cells. These reactions probably release substances that damage the cell. The result of too much ultraviolet light is sunburn, deep wrinkles, thickened skin, brown spots, and possibly skin cancer. In addition to damaging skin, ultraviolet light can cause damage to the eyes.

One way to protect yourself from sunburn is to use sunblock or sunscreen. These contain substances that either absorb or reflect ultraviolet wavelengths. Either action prevents most (but not all) of the damaging waves from reaching your skin.

▶ *Professor Plait suggests that an astronaut's skin could be protected from sunburn by a sunblock. Why might sunblock not be enough to prevent sunburn out in space?*

_____

_____

_____

▶ *What jobs here on Earth might expose people to more skin and eye damage than usual? (Hint: Damage is not only caused by lack of protection, but by spending long periods of time in bright sunlight.)*

_____

_____

▶ Take Action

CONDUCT AN INTERVIEW Sunburn greatly increases the risk of certain skin and eye cancers. For people who need to be outside all day every day, sunny weather can be a serious danger. Interview a lifeguard or someone else who works all day in the sun to find out what they do to protect their skin and eyes. Record what you find out below.

_____

_____

_____

_____

The Energy of Waves

Zapped Foods

Electromagnetic waves have uses as well as dangers.

If you buy fast-food burgers or chicken, you might have eaten food zapped with electromagnetic waves. Sound dangerous? It's actually been done to protect you. Over a century ago, scientists discovered that electromagnetic waves can be used to kill bacteria in food. Today, this process is becoming more and more common.

▶ Read

NOTEZONE

Underline the type of electromagnetic waves that can be used to kill bacteria.

What would you write in your diary if your dad was going to work in a place that "zapped" meat? Here's one writer's idea.

What's up with "zapped" foods?

Dear Diary,

Bad news! We have to move. My dad got a job...at [a] meat lab.... [H]e will be working with meat that is irradiated (ear-RAY-dee-ay-ted).... [H]e'll be using gamma rays to zap and kill bacteria in the meat. It's the bacteria that make people sick....

I asked my science teacher about irradiation.... He told me to look it up...and give a report to the class.... I did some research, and here's what I've written so far:

"Irradiation makes foods safe to eat by killing the bacteria in meat and poultry. It also kills trichina (trih-KY-nuh) worms in pork and insects in wheat, potatoes, flour, spices, tea, fruits, and vegetables...."

Foods aren't changed when they are irradiated. A raw apple stays crisp and juicy, and meat isn't cooked.... Of course the big question is—is it really safe?

FIND OUT MORE

SCIENCESAURUS

Characteristics of
  a Wave   306
Kinds of Waves   307
Electromagnetic
  Spectrum   309

Here's what I found out:

"The process can't be used on all foods, but it is used on many. It not only kills bacteria that will make you sick, but it also keeps foods fresh.... That means some foods don't need to be refrigerated after going through the irradiation process."

Amanda

---

irradiated: treated with electromagnetic radiation

bacteria: microscopic organisms, some of which cause diseases

trichina worms: tiny worms found in pork that can cause serious disease

From: Murphy, Dee. "What's Up with 'Zapped' Foods?" *Current Health*.

Explore

HOW DOES IT WORK? Gamma rays are one type of electromagnetic wave. Circle their position on the diagram on page 100.

Electromagnetic waves with higher frequencies carry more energy than those with lower frequencies.

▶ *Compared to other electromagnetic waves, are gamma rays high-energy or low-energy? Explain how you know.*

_____

_____

▶ *How is the energy in gamma waves used to make food safe?*

_____

_____

_____

In food irradiation plants, packaged food is placed on a moving belt that carries the food into a sealed room. There the food is exposed to gamma rays. Then the moving belt carries the food out of the room. All workers are carefully protected from getting anywhere near the gamma rays.

▶ *Why do you think the "zapping" is done by machines while people are far away?*

_____

_____

Sounding Off

BAD VIBRATIONS

Can you see sound?

Have you ever noticed an object shaking back and forth? Maybe you've seen a washing machine struggling through a spin cycle, or a tuning fork after it's been struck against someone's palm. If so, you've seen vibrations. Often, vibrating objects (such as violin strings) create sound waves. But sometimes sound waves cause objects to vibrate.

◄ **Tuning fork**

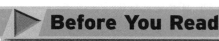

Before You Read

CAN YOU SEE WHAT YOU HEAR? A sound wave traveling through air is a vibration sensed by our ears. When sound travels through a liquid or solid we can sometimes see or feel the vibrations. Walls and windows don't have ears, but loud sounds can make them tremble. Try to remember a time you heard a sound so loud that you saw or felt something in your house vibrate.

► *Describe the sound and the objects you felt or saw vibrating.*

_____

_____

_____

_____

_____

_____

_____

_____

Underline ways that sound moved or changed matter in the reading.

Physics professor Walter Lewin showed a group of science teachers a way to see sounds.

A Shattering Sound

[Professor Lewin's presentation made] good use of both sight and sound, and touched a good many eardrums. Professor Lewin used...visual demonstrations...to explain sound waves. [T]hen...[he shattered] a wine glass with a loud, even tone....

...Sound is a pressure wave that compresses and decompresses the air to make a vibration.... [A vibration is] a disturbance that [spreads, like movement] through a [crowd] of people when one begins...shoving the next. When that pressure wave reaches your ear, the eardrum begins to vibrate at the same frequency, and your brain tells you something.

...[Sound can also be destructive when it makes an object] vibrate at a ... special frequency to which it is extremely sensitive.... [To demonstrate this,] Professor Lewin... rubbed a moistened finger around the rim of a wine glass to find the [special] tone, or frequency, ...of that glass. Then [he used] an electronic device to reproduce the tone at high volume. [This]...shattered the [glass] with sound waves.

---

compress: press together
decompress: push apart
frequency: the number of sound waves produced per second
moistened: wet

From: Brehm, Denise. "Lewin Shows Properties of Sound." Massachusetts Institute of Technology News Office. (web.mit.edu/newsoffice/tt/1998/jul15/conflewin.html)

FIND OUT MORE

SCIENCE SAURUS

Forms of Energy	300
Waves	305
Sound	312
Properties of Sound	313

SCI LINKS
THE WORLD'S A CLICK AWAY

www.scilinks.org
Keyword: Sound
Code: GSPD12

HOW DID HE DO IT? The diagram to the right shows what Professor Lewin's wine glass looked like just before it shattered. The dotted and solid lines show how the glass rim changed shape as it vibrated. The rim was pushed out of shape more and more as each second passed. After several seconds of the sound playing, the glass shattered.

▶ *Describe how sound was able to change the shape of the wine glass. Use information from the diagram in your answer.*

_____

_____

_____

▶ *How was sound able to shatter the glass?*

_____

_____

_____

MAKE INFERENCES

▶ *Energy is the ability to move or change matter. How did Professor Lewin demonstrate that sound is energy?*

_____

_____

_____

▶ *The reading states that Professor Lewin used sound at a high volume. What can you infer about the connection between the energy of the sound wave and the volume of the sound?*

_____

_____

_____

CREATE A MODEL

The sound in Professor Lewin's demonstration shattered the wine glass by causing the rim of the glass to quickly flex back and forth between a circular shape and an oval shape. Use the following model to see this effect in slow motion.

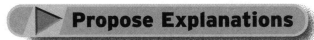

What You Need:
• 2 plastic foam coffee cups

What to Do:
1. Hold one cup upright between the palms of your hands. As slowly as you can, press your palms together, gently squishing the rim of the cup until opposite sides touch. Then slowly release the cup.
2. Turn the cup one-quarter turn and hold it between your palms again. Press your hands together very slowly until the rim is flattened.

▶ *What happened to the cup?*

_____

_____

3. Hold the second cup upright between the palms of your hands. Quickly clap your hands together, flattening the rim of the cup. Release the cup.
4. Turn the cup one-quarter turn and hold it between your palms again. Clap your hands together again quickly.
5. Repeat steps 3 and 4 five more times with the same cup.

▶ *What happened to the second cup?*

_____

_____

▶ Propose Explanations

▶ *In your model, what did your hands represent?*

_____

_____

▶ *Describe the pressure that caused the plastic foam cup to crack.*

_____

107

Sounding Off

GOOD VIBRATIONS

How do you tell the difference between music and noise?

You and your parents may disagree about what's music and what's noise. But the difference between music and noise is more than just a matter of opinion. It's a matter of mathematics and the shape of the sound waves. Long, stretched-out waves produce deep, low tones. Short, close-together waves produce higher pitched tones. How the different-shaped sound waves are combined determines whether a sound is musical or not.

 Before You Read

THINK ABOUT IT There are many different kinds of sounds. Some are pleasant to listen to, and some are not. Think about different kinds of sounds that are familiar to you. Decide if they are unpleasant or pleasant. List a few of the sounds in the circles below. Around the circles, list words or phrases that describe what makes these sounds pleasant or unpleasant.

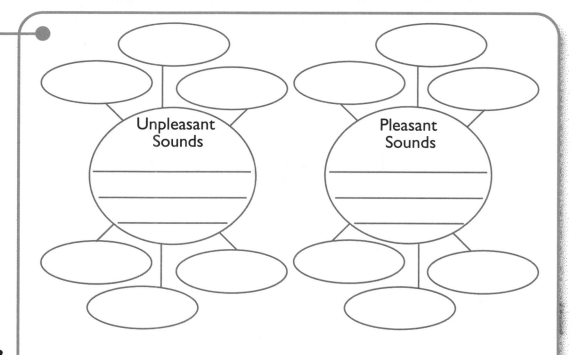

Unpleasant Sounds

Pleasant Sounds

▶ Read

What's the difference between drumming on a Caribbean steel pan and banging on kitchen pots? One is music and the other isn't. That's because master craftsmen carefully heat and pound the surface of a steel pan to form dimples that produce 28 distinct notes.

The Physics of Music

Engineers are still studying the intricacies of steel-pan music, but the basics are simple. Every musical tone has three traits: pitch—how high or low the note is; volume—how loud it is; and timbre—the "color" of the sound, which makes a note played on a steel pan different from the same note played on a trumpet. The sound is created when a source object (a note on the steel pan) is excited (hit) and made to vibrate. The pitch of the sound depends on its frequency—the numbers of times it vibrates per second—which is determined by the size, mass and other physical properties of the source. The bigger the source of the sound, the more room there is for the wave to form and the longer the wavelength will be. Longer wavelengths have lower frequencies, and when the sound waves reach us we hear a lower pitched note.

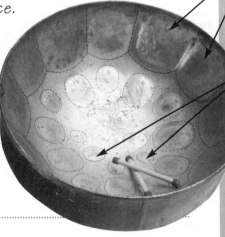

Lowest notes from largest dimples

Highest notes from smallest dimples

▲ Steel pan

frequency: the number of waves produced per second
wavelength: the distance between one point of a wave and the same point on the next wave

From: Miller, Jake. "The Physics of Music." *Scientific American Explorations.*

FIND OUT MORE

SCIENCESAURUS

Waves	305
Characteristics of a Wave	306
Sound	312
Properties of Sound	313

SCI**LINKS**
THE WORLD'S A CLICK AWAY

www.scilinks.org
Keyword: Sound
Code: GSPD12

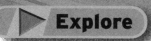

ANALYZE DATA When an object vibrates, it can create sound waves, which we hear as sounds. A sound's pitch (how high or low it is) depends on the frequency of the sound waves, or how many waves are produced per second. High-pitched sounds have high frequencies (many waves per second). Low-pitched sounds have low frequencies (fewer waves per second).

Some vibrating objects produce sound waves of different frequencies at the same time. Whether a sound is considered music or noise depends on whether there is a pattern among the frequencies. Hertz (Hz) is a unit of measure for frequency, just as meter is a unit of measure for distance. This table shows frequencies of sound waves made by two familiar objects. One of the objects is a musical instrument. The other is not.

Frequency of Sound Waves Produced	
Object 1	Object 2
200 Hz	197 Hz
400 Hz	211 Hz
600 Hz	217 Hz
800 Hz	219 Hz
1000 Hz	287 Hz
	311 Hz
	329 Hz
	399 Hz
	407 Hz

▶ *How are the two sets of frequencies different?*

_____

_____

▶ *Describe any pattern you see in the frequencies produced by the objects.*

_____

_____

MAKE INFERENCES

▶ *What can you infer about the sound made by the combinations of frequencies that each object produces? Which object probably makes the more musical sound?*

_____

_____

▶ *Which object do you think is a musical instrument? Explain your answer.*

_____

_____

_____

▶ Propose Explanations

COMPARE AND CONTRAST

▶ *How are noise and music alike? Explain your answer.*

_____

_____

_____

▶ *To one person, a set of sounds may seem like music. To another person, the same sounds seem like noise. What is one way to tell if a set of sounds is more like noise or music?*

_____

_____

_____

_____

▶ Take Action

WRITE A PARAGRAPH Think about the sounds made by your favorite musical instrument. Describe the instrument and the sounds it produces. Then describe the sounds in terms of their pitch, volume, and timbre. What do they make you think of? How do they make you feel?

_____

_____

_____

_____

_____

_____

_____

_____

Sounding Off

Healing Vibrations

Sound waves move or change matter—even matter inside a person's body!

Doctors often use high-frequency sound waves to make pictures of structures inside the human body. These waves are known as ultrasound. Like other sound waves, ultrasound waves contain energy. Recently, doctors have found a new way to make use of the energy contained in ultrasound waves.

 **Read**

NOTEZONE

Underline the three ways of treating internal wounds mentioned in the reading.

Doctors at the University of Washington are using sound waves to stop bleeding deep inside a patient's body.

STOP THE BLEEDING

There is no [easy way to] stop internal bleeding without surgery, which is...risky. As an alternative, some researchers are hoping to use ultrasound to [find], heat and cauterize internal wounds. But cooking tissue in that way is too dangerous if bleeding occurs in areas [like] the brain, or if the problem is hard to [find] and doctors need to treat a large area of the body.

Now a team from the University of Washington in Seattle has discovered that high-intensity focused ultrasound beams can [speed up] natural [blood] clotting, and stop bleeding without heating up tissue.

Sound waves make blood move around more than usual. This activates platelets by tricking them into thinking they are flowing through an open wound. [The platelets then] stick to membranes and each other. [This helps blood] clots to form.

[This] technique could be a...life-saving option when cauterizing is too dangerous. "We are really excited about [it]," says team member Lawrence Crum.

---

ultrasound: high-frequency sound waves beyond the range of human hearing
cauterize: stop bleeding by burning
high-intensity: high-energy

clotting: forming clots in blood to stop bleeding
platelets: small particles in the blood involved in clotting
membranes: thin layers of tissue that act as a lining

From: "Stop the Bleeding." *newscientist.com*
(www.newscientist.com/conferences/confarticle.jsp?conf=acsam200006&id=22411500)

FIND OUT MORE

SCIENCESAURUS

Circulatory
System   093
Waves   305
Characteristics
of a Wave   306

SCILINKS
THE WORLD'S A CLICK AWAY

www.scilinks.org
Keyword: Sound
Code: GSPD12

UNIT 3: SOUND, LIGHT, AND HEAT

Propose Explanations

MAKE INFERENCES

▶ *The passage describes two ways that ultrasound can be used to heal wounds. Explain how each method uses sound to move or change matter.*

_____

_____

_____

_____

Remember that sound is vibration, and frequency is a measure of how many vibrations occur per second. The human ear can only hear sounds within a certain range of frequencies, generally between 20 and 20,000 vibrations per second. The frequency of medical ultrasound can reach 10 million vibrations per second. The higher the rate of vibration, the more energy the sound wave carries.

▶ *Explain how ultrasound can burn tissue while the sound of a hair dryer cannot.*

_____

_____

_____

_____

_____

Take Action

WRITE A JOURNAL ENTRY Imagine that you are a scientist trying to come up with a new way to use sound energy. Think about how sound energy affects matter. In your journal, record your latest design idea. Explain what problem you are trying to solve and how your idea would use sound waves to solve it.

_____

_____

_____

_____

Light It Up!

SEEING NEAR AND FAR

What image comes to mind when you see the name Benjamin Franklin?

You might imagine a man in knee pants flying a kite in a lightning storm. But Ben Franklin is famous for more than investigating electricity. He was also a printer, inventor, city planner, and diplomat. As an elderly man, Franklin traveled back and forth between the American colonies and France seeking money and support for the American Revolution. During his time in France, he was inspired to improve his eyeglasses.

▲ **Ben Franklin**

▶ **Read**

NOTEZONE

Underline the problem Franklin had which led to his invention.

Always an inventor, here's what Franklin wrote to the man who made his eyeglasses back in Philadelphia.

Ben Franklin's Spectacles

I imagine it will be found pretty generally true, that the same convexity of glass, through which a man sees clearest and best at the distance proper for reading, is not the best for greater distances. I therefore had formerly two pair of spectacles, which I shifted occasionally, as in traveling I sometimes read, and often wanted to regard the prospects. Finding this change troublesome, and not always sufficiently ready, I had the glasses cut, and half of each kind [placed] in the same circle....

By this means, as I wear my spectacles constantly, I have only to move my eyes up or down, as I want to see distinctly far or near, the proper glasses being always ready. This I find more particularly convenient since my being in France, the glasses that serve me best at table to see what I eat, not being the best to see the faces of those on the other side of the

FIND OUT MORE

SCIENCESAURUS

| Light | 308 |
| Steps in Technology Design | 357 |

SCILINKS
THE WORLD'S A CLICK AWAY

www.scilinks.org
Keyword: Lenses
Code: GSPD13

table who speak to me; and when one's ears are not well
accustomed to the sounds of a language, a sight of the
movements in the features of him that speaks helps to
explain; so that I understand French better by the help of
my spectacles.

— Ben Franklin

convexity: curvature, or roundness
formerly: before

spectacles: eyeglasses
prospects: the view or scene
accustomed to: used to

From: a letter to George Whatley by Benjamin Franklin on May 23, 1785.

▶ Explore

BENDING LIGHT A lens is a curved piece of glass that bends light moving through it, helping to focus the light for people who don't see clearly. A convex (curved out) lens helps people to read up close. A concave (curved in) lens helps people see far.

Based on the reading, label the photograph of Ben's bifocal spectacles. Show which parts are used to see distant objects, and which are used to see nearby objects. Then label each lens "convex" or "concave."

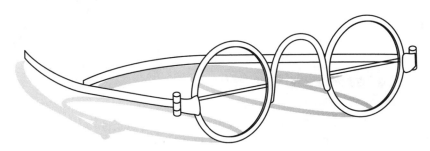

THE MOTHER OF INVENTION As the old saying goes, "Necessity is the mother of invention."

▶ *How does the saying fit the case of Ben Franklin's spectacles?*

_____

_____

_____

_____

_____

Light It Up!

SEEING COLORS

Your brain is pretty smart when it comes to seeing colors, but it can be fooled.

If you've seen a rainbow or shined a light through a glass prism, you know that white light is made up of all the colors of visible light. When white light, such as sunlight at midday, strikes an object, some of the colors of light are absorbed by the object. The remaining colors are reflected by the object. The colors of reflected light that enter your eyes are what gives an object its color.

Seems simple, doesn't it? Well, it's not. Scientists who study color and vision have to think about the brain as well as the eyes. Your brain acts like a powerful computer—analyzing color information sent from your eyes and, sometimes, getting fooled.

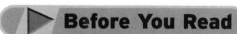

LIGHT EFFECTS Imagine you are served a slice of pizza with red tomatoes and green peppers in a brightly lit school cafeteria. Now imagine the same slice of pizza in a candle-lit restaurant. Now imagine it outside on a picnic table. How might the appearance of the pizza change from place to place?

_____

_____

_____

_____

_____

_____

UNIT 3: SOUND, LIGHT, AND HEAT

▶ Read

NOTEZONE

What questions do you have after reading this?

Tony Vladusich is a visual scientist from Australia. He is investigating how the brain knows what colors should look like under different lighting conditions.

COLOR IT IN

In the natural world, we see different [colors] depending on the wavelengths of light that are absorbed by and reflected from a surface. As illumination changes in the environment, for example from a midday sun to a reddish sunset, an object's [color], in theory, should also change. But it doesn't; things may seem a slightly different shade, but that's...[all]. ...[T]he fact that a blue book does not [change color] under different light indicates that the brain must have some mechanism to keep [colors] stable during changing environmental conditions....

It performs this feat by consulting its own... "[color] chart." This [system] works by looking at how two blobs of [color] contrast with each other, a factor that is constant whatever the lighting conditions.

"Essentially the brain takes notice of edges and boundaries between objects in the real world," Vladusich says. "It extracts that edge information, which is free from the effects of illumination, and fills the rest in.... It knows that light changes but contrast doesn't."

----

wavelength: the distance from the crest of one wave to the crest of the next wave; the colors of visible light vary in their wavelengths
absorbed: taken in
reflected: bounced off
illumination: lighting

mechanism: process
stable: unchanged
feat: act of skill
consulting: getting the advice of
extracts: pulls out
contrast: the difference between lighter and darker

From: "Colour Scheme." *Beyond 2000.* (www.beyond2000.com/news/Aug_00/story_721.html)

FIND OUT MORE

SCIENCESAURUS
Light   308
Electromagnetic
  Spectrum   309
Light at a Surface   311

SCI LINKS.
THE WORLD'S A CLICK AWAY

www.scilinks.org
Keyword: Light and Color
Code: GSPD14

COLOR CONSTANCY Picture a bowl of lemons and limes outside on a picnic table at sundown. During a reddish sunset, the red light from the sun makes the lemons look orange. But the red light also makes the green limes next to the lemons look different. The brain notices how the lemons and limes contrast, and "sees" them as the same colors they would appear in the midday sunlight. So the brain holds these colors "constant," or the same, even when the light reflected from them has changed.

▶ *Imagine looking at a piece of white chalk on a colored background on a very bright sunny day. Now imagine how the chalk might look as a dark cloud moved overhead. Would the chalk still reflect the same colors of light? Would it still look the same color to your brain? Explain.*

_____

_____

_____

FOOLING THE BRAIN As the brain tries to determine what color an object is, it takes in color information about more than just the single object. Background colors are also part of the picture the brain sees.

▶ *Compare the two pictures below. How is the color of the bricks different?*

_____

_____

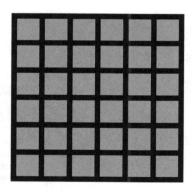   

If you said the bricks on the left are darker, you are not alone. But the color of the bricks is exactly the same in both pictures.

▶ *Explain why you think the bricks on the left look darker.*

_____

_____

_____

BEFORE AND AFTER

Try this to get your brain to "see" what isn't there!

What You Need: set of colored markers

What to Do:
1. Color the stop sign on the left, making the space around the letters red.
2. Hold this book at arm's length. Stare at the stop sign for 30 seconds.
3. Then stare at the blank stop sign on the right.
4. Color the stop sign on the right the way it appeared to you.

 Propose Explanations

WHICH RECEPTORS? There are three kinds of color receptor cells in your eye. Each kind is sensitive to a different range of wavelengths of light. One kind can sense mostly red light, one mostly blue light, and the third mostly green light. If the light reflected from an object is mostly in the red wavelengths, the red color cells will send a stronger signal to the brain than the other receptor cells. The brain compares the strengths of all three signals and "sees" a color.

When color receptors get a strong signal for a long time, they become tired. Then they stop sending messages about that color to the brain.

▶ *In the activity, which color receptor cells do you think got tired?*

_____

An afterimage is the image you see after you stop looking at a real object. When you look at a white page, all colors of light are reflected into your eyes. If your red-sensitive cells are still tired, no red signal is sent to the brain. However, the other two signals are still strong.

▶ *Use this information to explain what you saw when you looked at the blank stop sign.*

_____

_____

Light It Up!

MAGIC MIRRORS

Can you believe it? It's a living human head without a body!

Penn and Teller, a team of humorous magicians, can fool almost anyone with their illusions and sleight of hand. In one famous magic trick, Penn explains that Teller lost his head in a car accident. Penn tells the audience that through the wonders of modern medicine, doctors have been able to keep Teller's head alive. Finishing his story, Penn pulls away a cloth. The audience suddenly sees Teller's head—living, breathing, talking, and not attached to a body!

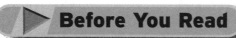 **Before You Read**

▲ **A student demonstrates Penn and Teller's "floating head" trick.**

THINK ABOUT IT If you stand in a totally dark room, you can't see a thing. You need light to see your book, your dog, and your best friend. None of these things gives off their own light. So, how can you see them? They reflect light from the sun or some other light source. Some objects reflect light in a more ordered way than others. When you look into these objects—such as calm water or a mirror—you see a reflection.

▶ *Think about reflections you have seen. Describe one below.*

_____

_____

_____

▶ *How far away was the object from the surface that reflected it? How far away did the object's reflection seem to be from the surface?*

_____

_____

_____

_____

246

NOTEZONE

Underline two facts about reflecting light that make Penn and Teller's trick possible.

Backstage, the magicians explain the science behind their magic.

MAGIC:
THE SCIENCE OF ILLUSION

Backstage at this illusion...Penn admits that medical science isn't keeping Teller's head alive. Optics, the science of mirrors, drives this illusion.

A large mirror propped in front of Teller's body leaves his head visible. The predictable properties of mirrors— light bounces off it at the same angle it arrives, and a mirror image appears as far behind the mirror as the real thing is in front—let us set up the mirror to control what you see.

The mirror is exactly between the front and the back walls, which are painted the same. So while you think you're looking under Teller's head to the back wall, you're really seeing a reflection of the front wall. And the checkered floor helps the illusion too, with the lines coming closer together in the "distance" just as you'd expect. The story of Teller's accident and the art of Penn & Teller's performance make the illusion complete.

....
predictable: expected

From: "Living Head Backstage." *Magic, the Science of Illusion.* California ScienCenter. (www.magicexhibit.org/illusions/illusions_LH_backstage.html)

FIND OUT MORE

SCIENCESAURUS
Properties of Light 310
Light at a Surface 311

TAKE ANOTHER LOOK To the audience, it looks like Teller's head was cut off and placed on a table. But you know it can't be true. Taking a look from another angle helps us understand how the illusion is done. The diagram shows a view of the exhibit from the side.

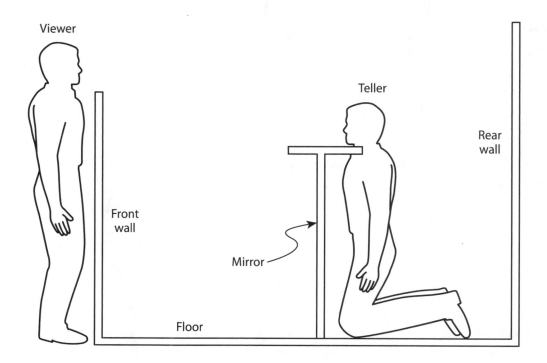

Penn and Teller know that in order to see a real object you must have a line of sight reaching it. (A line of sight is the straight line between the viewer's eyes and the object.) In this illusion, Teller's head is the real object.

▶ *On the diagram, draw a dotted line of sight from the viewer's eye to Teller's head.*

CHECK THE ANGLE The viewer can't see Teller's body because it is behind a large flat mirror. When the viewer looks at the mirror, he or she sees a reflected image of what's in front of the mirror.

▶ *On the diagram, draw a dashed line of sight from the viewer's eye to the top part of the mirror—about level with Teller's chest.*
▶ *Use a protractor to measure the angle made by your dashed line and the top half of the mirror.*
▶ *Then draw another dashed line from the top part of the mirror to make an equal angle with the bottom half of the mirror. The place where the second dashed line ends is the end of the line of sight.*

▶ *Where does the line of sight end? What will the viewer see?*

_____

_____

▶ *Draw a solid line of sight to a point in the lower part of the mirror—about level with Teller's hand. Measure the angle and draw where the line of sight ends up.*

▶ *Where does the line of sight end? What will the viewer see?*

_____

_____

▶ *No matter where the viewer looks in the mirror what will he or she see?*

_____

Penn and Teller also know that, to the viewer, each object seen in a mirror appears to be the same distance behind the mirror as it really is in front of the mirror.

▶ *So, what does the viewer think he is seeing when he actually sees the front wall in the mirror?*

_____

▶ *What does the viewer think he is seeing when he actually sees the floor in front of Teller in the mirror?*

_____

▶ Propose Explanations

COMPLETING THE ILLUSION Penn tells the audience a long story about how Teller lost his head in a car accident.

▶ *How does the story help create the illusion for the viewer?*

_____

_____

_____

_____

Heating Things Up

Head in the Clouds

Floating in a balloon, the sky's the limit.

Balloons were the first aircraft. In the 1700s, hot air lifted explorers skyward—but the balloons couldn't stay up long. In the 1800s, scientists experimented with lighter hydrogen gas to lift balloons. But hydrogen was dangerously explosive! Still, courageous balloonists never quit trying to improve their flights. In the year 2002, adventurer Steve Fossett used the newest balloon technology to become the first person ever to fly solo around the world in a hot-air balloon.

▶ **Before You Read**

RECALL EXPERIENCES Balloons filled with hot air rise because hot air is lighter than cool air. Can you think of different places where you have seen hot air rising or knew that hot air was rising?

_____

_____

_____

_____

_____

_____

_____

_____

_____

_____

_____

UNIT 3: SOUND, LIGHT, AND HEAT

124

The author writes as if the sun and the balloon were living things.

(Circle) the two verbs that describe the balloon's or sun's actions in terms of human feelings.

The first hot-air balloon flight occurred in 1783, and lasted only a few minutes. But in 1784, French physicist Pilatre de Rozier had a better idea—a balloon that could keep its gases hot longer, and fly farther. Don Cameron, a modern balloon manufacturer, adopted Rozier's design—and the rest was history.

Steady as She Goes

Unlike air, a light gas such as hydrogen (or...helium) remains light without the constant [use] of fuel. Yet it, too, rises when heated and sinks when cooled. That's where burners and hot air can come in handy.

"The secret of making a gas balloon fly [for] long periods is to keep the helium the same temperature day and night," says Alan Noble, director of special projects for Cameron Balloons. "The problem is that during the day the sun is trying to warm it and at night it wants to radiate heat into the blackness of space. Our job is to keep the temperature as stable as possible." Cameron's so-called Rozier design places [two helium-filled balloons] above...air heated by propane. To [rise up], the aeronauts heat the air..., which in turn heats and expands the helium. The balloon's outer envelope consists of two layers, and the dead air space between the layers cuts heat loss at night by 50 percent. During the day the sun takes over to warm the helium, but should the balloon want to rise..., solar-powered fans can draw in cool air so that the temperature inside remains stable. "It's what we call air conditioning...," Noble says. It's also what you would call a success: the majority of distance and duration flights have been flown in Cameron-built Roziers....

----

radiate: send out
propane: a type of fuel

aeronaut: someone who travels in a balloon

From: "The Balloon that Flew Around the World." *Scientific American.com*
(www.sciam.com/article.cfm?co1ID=1&article1D=000CF318-089B-1C74-9B81809EC588EF21)

FIND OUT MORE

SCIENCESAURUS
Properties of
  Matter   251
States of Matter 253
Temperature
  versus Heat   302
Methods of Heat
  Transfer   304

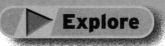
INTERPRET AN ENGINEERING DIAGRAM When engineering teams create new products, they first make plans of their design. They must think of all the details and requirements that will make their product work, and include these in their plans. These are called specifications. Making diagrams helps engineers communicate their ideas clearly. The diagrams must show how a design meets the specifications to build the product.

► *Below is a diagram of the Rozier balloon. For each labeled part of the diagram, add a note that tells what its purpose is. Remember that a Rozier balloon needs:*

1. A source of heat
2. A system for cooling
3. A warm air pocket
4. A layer of dead air to insulate
5. Lighter-than-air gas

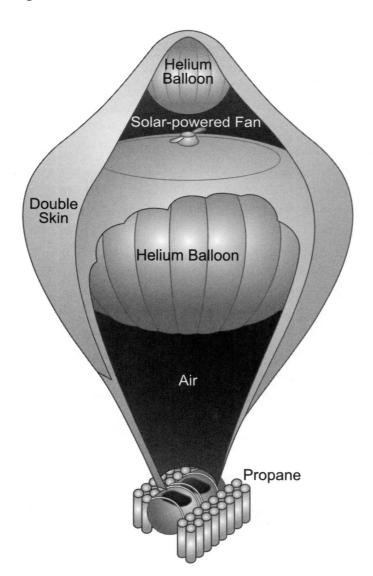

THINK ABOUT IT Balloonists cannot steer a balloon. The only way their direction changes is when air currents push the balloon. Air currents move in different directions at different elevations.

► *Explain how balloonists might use their fans or heaters to change direction.*

_____

_____

_____

_____

► Take Action

BRIGHT IDEAS When inventors get good ideas, they describe them very carefully in a request for a "patent." A patent is a formal record kept on file by the government that proves an idea is yours. If someone else were to later come up with the same idea, they would search the files at the United States Patent Office and find that you thought of it first.

► *Imagine you are working for Pilatre de Rozier. Your scientific team is filling out an application for a patent on the design for the Rozier balloon. In order to be given a patent on your invention, you need to show that it is a significant improvement over what already exists. Describe how the Rozier design is better than a simple, single balloon filled with hot air or helium. Remember to use scientific terms found in the passage.*

PATENT APPLICATION

_____

_____

_____

_____

_____

_____

_____

Heating Things Up

Can You Feel the HEAT?

How did that pie filling get so hot?

Have you ever put a little frozen pie in the toaster oven for a couple of minutes, and then taken a quick bite? The crust may not have felt too hot on the tongue, but when you bite into the filling—ouch! Some foods feel hotter than others. What do you need to know to keep from getting burned?

NOTEZONE

Circle the two different principles involved in the process of burning your tongue.

Underline what each principle measures.

FIND OUT MORE

SCIENCESAURUS

SCI LINKS.
THE WORLD'S A CLICK AWAY

www.scilinks.org
Keyword: Heat Transfer
Code: GSPD15

 **Read**

Here's a tasty science lesson with a moral for anyone who has ever burned their tongue.

HOT STUFF

Question: Why is an apple pie's sauce always hotter than the pastry even though they have been cooked on the same heat?

Answer: The paradox you describe arises from the [use] of the word "hotter." As you point out, the pastry and filling have been resting in the same oven for long enough to come to the same temperature – and therefore one is not hotter than the other in this sense....

Despite the temperatures being equal, your tongue is still more likely to get burned by the filling than the crust, though. There are 2 principles behind this: thermal conductivity and specific heat capacity.

Thermal conductivity is just the measure of how quickly heat energy travels through a substance. The pastry contains many pockets of air and cannot [conduct] energy...to...your tongue [easily]....

Specific heat capacity...measures how much [heat] energy must be contained in a substance for it to have a certain temperature... For example, 100 grams of aluminum at 100 degrees C has more heat [energy] than 100 grams of copper at the same temperature.... Since the [pie] filling is mostly made of water, and water has a very high specific heat, the filling has a lot of heat to give off [before its temperature drops. So] when the pie comes out of the oven, the filling cools down much more slowly….

The long and short of it is—stick to ice cream—it's safer!

paradox: something that doesn't seem to make sense

principles: reasons

thermal conductivity: the ability of a substance to let heat energy pass through it

specific heat capacity: the amount of heat energy a substance needs to change temperature

From: Landolfi, Rob. *PhysLink.com.* (www.physlink.com/Education/AskExperts/ae463.cfm)

▶ Explore

TAKE THE HEAT Different materials need different amounts of heat energy to warm up. The amount of heat energy needed to warm a substance by 1°C is the property called specific heat.

The excerpt tells you that 100 grams of aluminum at 100°C has more heat energy than the same amount of copper at the same temperature.

▶ *Which material has a higher specific heat, copper or aluminum? How do you know?*

_____

_____

_____

Think about two different saucepans. Both are the same shape and have the same mass. One saucepan is made of copper and the other is made of aluminum. Say that you put both saucepans into the oven and heated them to 200°C.

▶ *Which of the two saucepans would get hot faster? Explain your reasoning in terms of specific heat.*

_____

_____

▶ *When you removed the two saucepans from the oven, which would take longer to cool down? Explain your reasoning in terms of specific heat.*

_____

_____

_____

Heating Things Up

SOME LIKE IT HOT

Brrr! Do you like to stay warm in cold weather? You don't have to shear a sheep to do it.

Humans have used wool, leather, cotton, and linen to make their clothing for thousands of years. Natural materials work fine for some activities. But get a wool sweater wet and it could shrink. It might even smell sheepish. Today's designers often use new kinds of materials. Synthetic, or man-made, fabrics are common choices for making clothing. Some synthetics you might have seen before include acrylic, polyester, and rayon.

▶ **Before You Read**

WHAT'S IN A LABEL? Believe it or not, many of the clothes we wear are made from materials that start out as oil. Chemical engineers make plastics from oil-related materials. Liquid plastic gets drawn out into thin threads or fibers. Then machines weave or knit the fibers into fabrics. These fabrics can keep us warmer, cooler, drier, and more comfy than natural materials.

▶ *Look at the labels from the clothes you are wearing today. Write down all the materials listed. Circle any that are synthetic.*

_____

_____

_____

_____

_____

NOTEZONE

Imagine you are writing an ad to sell Polartec.® (Circle) four words or phrases you might use in your ad.

What's cozier than a heavy wool coat? Just ask the folks at the Malden Mills fabric company.

It's Fuzzy Wuzzy Time

Forget Dolly, the infamous test-tube lamb cloned by Scottish scientists. Aaron Feuerstein and the folks at Malden Mills began building a better sheep way back in the 1970s. And what a sheep they built. Their invention, a fuzzy polyester fabric first called Polarfleece®, changed the way backcountry enthusiasts dress for the outdoors.

It all started when …[Feuerstein] encouraged his research and development team to experiment with synthetic alternatives to wool. Pile fabrics made from [man-made materials] had just hit the scene, and their future looked promising…Malden's team set out to develop a durable but lightweight fabric that would dry quickly, stretch slightly for a more forgiving fit than wool, and accept a variety of dyes. Like good Argonauts, they returned with a fleece [that had] magical properties. Their brainchild was a single-sided polyester material with a fleecy finish that trapped heat as efficiently as wool and fibers that didn't absorb water, shrink, or stink after intense use…. Malden's Polartec® line…now boasts 150 fabrics, including a variety of fleeces designed to handle all sorts of outdoor activities and weather conditions.

So three cheers for the fuzzy stuff. Thanks to an enterprising fabric company, we stay warm and the sheep stay happy.

---

infamous: famous but unpopular
enthusiasts: people who spend a lot of time at an activity
pile: soft and velvety
durable: tough
Argonauts: characters in a Greek story who sailed the world looking for a magical ram with a golden wooly coat

fleece: a sheep's coat of wool, or a fabric that looks like that
efficiently: well
boasts: includes
enterprising: hard-working

From: Dorn, Jonathan. "Polartec: Building a Better Sheep." *Backpacker.*

FIND OUT MORE

SCIENCESAURUS

Temperature versus Heat	302
Methods of Heat Transfer	304

SC**I**LINKS.
THE WORLD'S A CLICK AWAY

www.scilinks.org
Keyword: Insulation
Code: GSPD16

THAT FLEECE IS GOLDEN Your body generates heat energy, but it has trouble staying warm in very cold weather. That's because heat energy is transferred from warmer objects to cooler objects. If you put your hand on a cold windowpane, the glass draws heat energy away from your hand and cools your hand down. In the same way, cold air takes heat energy from your body.

Clothing helps to stop your body's heat energy from escaping to the cold air. There is a thin but important layer of air between your skin and your clothing. Air is a very good insulator (a material that does not transfer heat energy easily). So, this layer of air helps trap your body's warmth.

▶ *Why would it be smart to wear several layers of clothes in very cold weather?*

_____

_____

_____

Polartec® is specially designed to trap body warmth. The picture shows a close-up of how the fibers of Polartec® fabric are arranged.

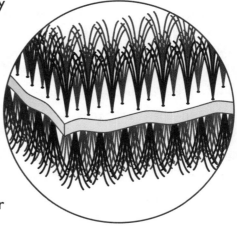

▶ *What do you see that makes Polartec® a good insulator?*

_____

_____

In Lesson 34 you read about a balloon designed to keep helium pockets warm for a long time.

▶ *Look carefully at the picture of the Rozier balloon on page 126. Which part of the balloon design helps keep heat energy trapped in the helium balloons?*

_____

_____

▶ *In this lesson you read about a fabric designed to keep warm bodies warm. How is the Rozier balloon design similar to the Polartec® fabric design?*

_____

_____

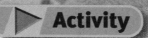

KEEPING WARM

Which glove will keep your hands toastier?

What You Need:

- pitcher of warm water
- thermometer
- measuring cup
- three resealable plastic bags
- one wool glove
- one Polartec® or other synthetic pile fabric glove
- access to a freezer

What to Do:

1. Fill a pitcher with warm water and put a thermometer in the water.
2. Read the thermometer and record the *Beginning Water Temperature.*
3. Measure and pour $\frac{1}{2}$ cup of water into each bag. Close bags tightly.
4. Fit one bag deeply into each glove.
5. Leave the third bag as a control, without a glove.
6. Place the two gloves and the control bag in a freezer for about 30 minutes.
7. Remove the gloves and the control bag from the freezer.
8. Open each bag one at a time and measure the temperature of the water inside. Record the *Ending Water Temperature* in the chart.

Beginning Water Temperature (°C) _____		
Type of Glove	**Ending Water Temperature (°C)**	**Temperature Change (°C)**
Natural material		
Synthetic material		
No glove (control)		

DRAW CONCLUSIONS

▶ *Which of the bags had the coldest water after being in the freezer?*

_____

▶ *Based on your results, what difference does wearing gloves in a cold environment make?*

_____

▶ *Which of the two gloves would keep your hands warmer? What evidence do you have for your answer?*

_____

_____

_____

UNIT 4 Matter

Matter is all the physical "stuff" around you.
Your shoes, the walls of your classroom, the teeth in the mouth of your pet hamster, even the tiny invisible molecules of air you breathe in and out are all made up of bits of matter. For thousands of years, philosophers and scientists around the world have been trying to describe what matter is and how it combines with other matter.

In this unit you'll take a look at some of the ways matter is described and classified. You'll find out how the model of the atom has changed over the centuries. You'll learn what the melting point of sand is, and what makes a perfect snow globe. You'll even determine whether or not a fictional *Star Trek* creature could actually exist.

Did You Know?
If you could throw a snowball fast enough, it would completely vaporize when it hit a brick wall.

Building Blocks

WHAT'S AN ATOM?

What happens when you divide the indivisible?

Just as letters are the units that make up words, sentences, and paragraphs, atoms are the units that make up elements, compounds, and all other kinds of matter. You can break a paragraph down into the single letters that make it up. But you can't break down a letter into anything smaller, or else it isn't a letter anymore! Likewise, you can break matter down into smaller and smaller pieces right down to a single atom. But atoms cannot be broken down into anything smaller without losing the special properties that give them their identity.

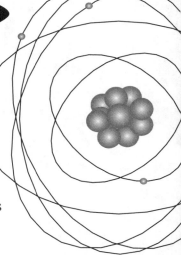

 **Activity**

DIVIDING ATOMS

See what happens when you try to divide an atom.

What You Need:
- assorted rubber bands (different sizes and colors)
- scissors

What to Do:
1. Begin with a handful of assorted rubber bands. This will represent a collection of different atoms.
2. Sort the rubber bands into piles so that all rubber bands in each pile are the same size and color.
3. Choose the largest pile. Divide it into two smaller piles.
4. Separate one of these two small piles into two smaller piles.
5. Continue dividing until your pile can't be divided any more.

What Do You See?

► *What do you have in your last pile?*

_____

► *What would you need to do in order to divide this last pile?*

_____

Go ahead and divide your last pile using the method you just described.

▷ Propose Explanations

CHANGING IDENTITIES Review the results of the activity on page 136.

▶ *How was the method you used to divide the last pile different from the method you used to divide the other piles?*

_____

_____

_____

_____

▶ *What property of rubber bands was lost when you divided your last pile?*

_____

_____

EVALUATING THE MODEL In the activity, you made a model of the individual atoms that make up elements (pure substances).

▶ *What represented a group of different elements in your model?*

_____

▶ *What represented a single element in your model?*

_____

▶ *What represented a single atom in your model?*

_____

An atom is the smallest part of an element that still has the properties of that element.

▶ *How does your model demonstrate this fact?*

_____

_____

_____

_____

_____

FIND OUT MORE

SCIENCESAURUS

Atoms	255
Atomic Structure	256
Atomic Size	257
Elements, Molecules, and Compounds	259
Elements	260

SCiLINKS
THE WORLD'S A CLICK AWAY

www.scilinks.org
Keyword: Molecules
and Atoms
Code: GSPD17

137

Building Blocks

Democritus's Tiny Particles

The idea that matter is made up of tiny particles is far from new.

When you hear someone talk about "atomic science," you may think of cutting-edge research. But the study of atoms goes back a long way. In fact, the word *atom* was first used almost 2,500 years ago. It comes from a Greek word that means "not divisible."

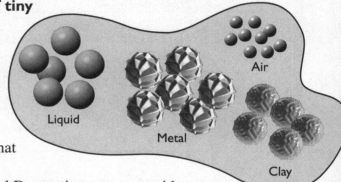

▲ **Democritus's atoms**

Around 440 B.C., a Greek scholar named Democritus came up with the idea that all matter is made up of tiny particles he called atoms. He imagined atoms as tiny, hard spheres that could not be broken apart. His was the first model of the atom. Our understanding of these small bits of matter has changed since then, but Democritus was right about some things.

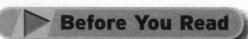
▶ Before You Read

TOO SMALL TO STUDY One way that scientists study things that are too small to be seen or too large to fit into a laboratory is to use models. For example, a map can show the whole world on a tabletop. An architect might make a model of a building she wants to construct. In Lesson 37 you made your own model of atoms and elements.

▶ *What other models can you think of that might be used to help people study something that cannot be seen easily?*

_____

_____

_____

_____

_____

▶ **Read**

Underline words or phrases that tell how Democritus imagined the physical properties of atoms.

Democritus believed that the physical properties of atoms could explain the behavior of different materials.

An Early Model

As we do today, Democritus imagined that there were many different kinds of atoms. Some, he said, are very light and free to dart about this way and that, and they can move far apart from each other. The air and other gases are made of such atoms, Democritus said.

But water had different kinds of atoms, thought Democritus, and they were arranged differently. He pictured the atoms of water and other liquids as larger and heavier than atoms of gases, because the atoms of liquids tend to stick together. And since anyone could see that liquids flow, their atoms must be slick and smooth. If they were not, they would not slip and slide over and around each other.

Atoms that make up copper, iron, rocks, and other heavy solid objects must be even larger and heavier than atoms of liquids, Democritus thought. And since it is hard to break apart such solid objects, their atoms must have very rough and jagged surfaces that cause the atoms to lock together tightly.

....

dart: move quickly   **slick:** slippery

From: Gallant, Roy. *Explorers of the Atom.* Doubleday.

FIND OUT MORE

SCIENCESAURUS

The Evolution of
  Atomic Theory   258
Elements, Molecules,
  and Compounds 259

SCI**LINKS**.
THE WORLD'S A CLICK AWAY

www.scilinks.org
Keyword: Molecules
  and Atoms
Code: GSPD17

A MODERN MODEL Democritus's idea that matter is made up of atoms is still accepted. But today, we know atoms are made of even smaller particles. These particles are protons, neutrons, and electrons. What makes one atom different from another isn't the texture of an atom's surface, it's the number of particles in the atom.

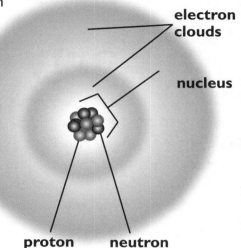

electron clouds

nucleus

proton   neutron

If you look at the drawing of an atom shown here, you will see that the particles we call protons and neutrons are in the center of the atom. This is the nucleus of the atom. Almost all of an atom's mass is contained in the nucleus. The number of protons and neutrons is about equal in most atoms. The particles we call electrons zip around through empty space, orbiting the nucleus in electron clouds. Most of the time the number of electrons is also equal to the number of protons.

In the modern model, it is the electrons in an atom's outermost electron cloud that interact with other atoms.

► *In what ways does the modern model agree with Democritus's ideas about the surface of the atom? In what ways is it different?*

_____

_____

_____

It wasn't until many centuries after Democritus lived that scientists first started conducting experiments with atoms in the laboratory. In one such experiment, protons were fired at a very, very thin sheet of gold foil. Most of the protons went straight through the foil and out the other side. But a few bounced back.

► *Use the model of the atom above to try to explain the results of this experiment.*

_____

_____

_____

_____

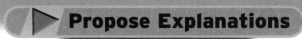

COMPARING METHODS Back in Democritus's time, scientists did not perform experiments and collect data. Instead, they simply thought about questions—debating and arguing their opinions with one another. Today, scientists rely on scientific evidence for answers to their questions.

▶ *Look back at the reading. What did Democritus base his ideas about atoms on?*

_____

_____

Democritus made an assumption about materials and the atoms that make them up that turned out to be incorrect.

▶ *What was the assumption?*

_____

_____

_____

Think about the gold foil experiment described on page 140.

▶ *How are the methods used by scientists today better than those used by philosophers in Democritus's time?*

_____

_____

_____

_____

▶ *What do modern scientists have that might have helped Democritus come up with a more accurate model of the atom?*

_____

_____

_____

_____

Democritus ▶

Building Blocks

Molecule Madness

Look out! The molecules are falling!

It's wonderful to stand outside and watch snowflakes collect on your outstretched arm. Snowflakes are delicate, six-sided crystals. Each crystal is made up of smaller ice crystals. And each ice crystal is built from a huge number of water molecules arranged just so. Scientists can actually calculate just how many molecules of water there are in a single snowflake.

Molecules are groups of linked atoms. In living things, most molecules contain atoms of carbon, hydrogen, and oxygen. Many molecules have a few other atoms linked on as well. Exactly how the atoms are arranged makes all the difference between one substance and another.

▲ **Microscopic view of a snowflake**

Before You Read

A STRATEGY FOR COUNTING It takes a long time to count a large group of objects. Sometimes you lose count in the middle, and have to start all over. What's the best way to count a large number of similar objects?

▶ *Suppose you have a big bag of paper clips and want to know how many are inside. How would you go about finding the total number?*

_____

_____

_____

_____

_____

_____

▶ **Read**

Science writer Kathy Wollard describes the molecules that make up a snowflake.

Countless Particles Make a Flake

How many molecules are in a single snowflake? And what is a molecule, anyway?

A molecule is what you get when atoms link up. There are only slightly more than 100 kinds of atoms in the universe.... A molecule can be made of several atoms (like a molecule of water) or hundreds of billions of atoms (like a molecule of DNA).

Some molecules we know and love: the oxygen we breathe, simply made of two oxygen atoms, linked together. Water, which is made of one oxygen atom linked to two hydrogen atoms. Table sugar, which is made of 12 carbon atoms, 22 hydrogen atoms and 11 oxygen atoms....

Which brings us to snowflakes. A snowflake is made of frozen crystals of water (leaving aside the bits of dirt the crystals may have frozen around). If we know how many water molecules are in an average snow crystal (about 1,000,000,000,000,000,000), and the number of snow crystals in an average snowflake (let's say 100), we can calculate the number of molecules in a flake.

The answer: about 100,000,000,000,000,000,000, or 100 quintillion water molecules. If someone sat you down to count the molecules in a snowflake, you couldn't finish in a million lifetimes.

DNA: the molecule that carries genetic information
crystals: solids whose molecules are arranged in a repeating pattern

From: Wollard, Kathy. "Countless Particles Make a Flake." *Newsday.*

Circle the atoms that make up a water molecule.

Underline the number of water molecules in a single snowflake.

FIND OUT MORE

SCIENCESAURUS
DNA   115
Elements, Molecules,
   and Compounds   259
Molecules   261
Scientific Notation 377

SCiLINKS
THE WORLD'S A CLICK AWAY

www.scilinks.org
Keyword: Molecules
   and Atoms
Code: GSPD17

TRY SCIENTIFIC NOTATION When you are counting atoms or molecules, there are a lot of zeros to write! It can be hard to work with numbers so large. So scientists don't write all those zeros. Instead, they use scientific notation to write large numbers. In scientific notation, a large number is written as a small number multiplied by a power of ten. An exponent is the raised number that tells how many times to multiply by ten.

   For example, to write 10,000 in scientific notation, you show how many times 1 is multiplied by 10 by writing 1×10^4. It may not be so hard to write the zeros in 10,000. But look again at the reading.

▶ *How many zeros are in the number of molecules in a snow crystal?*

_____

What happens if the number doesn't start with a 1? Put the decimal point after the first number. Then count the places after the decimal. That becomes the exponent you write after the 10. A single drop of water contains 280,000,000,000,000,000,000 molecules of water. In scientific notation, that's 2.8×10^{20} molecules. Now do you see why scientists use this shorter form for writing large numbers?

▶ *Complete the table below. Use information from the reading to fill in the number of molecules. (The last one has been done for you.) Then write each number in scientific notation.*

Object	Number of Molecules	Scientific Notation
Snow crystal		
Snowflake		
Drop of water		
A 100-pound person	917,000,000,000,000,000,000,000,000	

▶ *Which contains more molecules, a drop of water or a snow crystal? What's the easiest way to compare the numbers?*

_____

_____

_____

_____

_____

_____

GOT A HEADACHE? Scientists sometimes use molecules found in nature as models for new molecules they design in the laboratory. For example, people have known for thousands of years that the bark of the white willow tree could take away headache pain. Chemists studied the molecules in white willow bark to find the one that eased headaches. They then learned to make the molecule, which we now call aspirin, in the laboratory.

Many people find that aspirin upsets their stomachs. Chemists worked to make a similar substance that would not upset the stomach, but would still cure a headache. Acetaminophen is what they came up with.

Aspirin

Acetaminophen

Study the diagrams of the aspirin and acetaminophen molecules.

▶ *What do the two molecules have in common?*

_____

_____

Fill in the table to show how many of each type of atom make up one molecule of each pain reliever.

Molecule	Carbon Atoms	Hydrogen Atoms	Oxygen Atoms	Nitrogen Atoms
Aspirin				
Acetaminophen				

▶ *Based on the numbers in the table, how do the aspirin and acetaminophen molecules differ?*

_____

_____

Aspirin and acetaminophen are very similar molecules. Yet they are different substances with significantly different effects on the human body.

▶ *What can you conclude about the structure of molecules and the properties of the substances they make up?*

_____

_____

It's a Matter of State

FROG ANTIFREEZE

How cold does it get before you reach for a jacket?

Do you live in an area where temperatures fall below freezing in the winter? Does it get cold enough to freeze lakes and ponds? If so, you probably have heard of antifreeze for cars. Antifreeze keeps the water in the radiator from freezing into solid ice. If the water were to freeze, it could no longer be pumped around to cool the engine. Since water expands when it freezes into ice, the radiator could also be cracked open.

Cars in cold climates clearly need antifreeze. But have you ever heard of antifreeze for animals?

▶ **Before You Read**

IT'S COLD OUTSIDE You can go indoors and stay warm if it is freezing outside. But think about the animals that live where you are. Do you see the same animals all year long? How do you think wild animals in cold climates survive winter's freezing weather?

_____

_____

_____

_____

_____

_____

_____

_____

_____

▶ **Gray treefrog**

NOTEZONE

<u>Underline</u> how freezing temperatures can be dangerous to living things.

Jot down something that reading this made you curious about.

What's a frog-cicle? It's sort of like an icicle, but not quite.

Frog-cicles

[A] bunch of amphibians, all frogs…employ a pretty amazing trick to get through winter. The wood frog, boreal chorus frog, spring peeper, gray treefrog and Cope's gray treefrog don't bother to avoid the cold; they freeze solid and survive! As winter approaches, these frogs find a comfy spot on the forest floor, under some leaves or beneath a log, or under matted grass in a meadow, and just sit there. Next to the ground, with a protective blanket of snow above, the temperatures can often remain above freezing for much of the winter. But eventually they will dip below 0°C.

When temperatures drop below freezing, as much as 65% of the frog's body water is frozen into ice. But the frogs have a special trick to protect their individual cells from the effects of freezing:

[The frogs] arm themselves with antifreeze to protect their [cells]. Cold itself is not what harms living tissues and kills animals; it's the formation of ice crystals that tear up individual cells in tissues, causing death. These frogs flood their cells with glucose, a natural body sugar. This prevents the formation of ice-crystals, similar to what windshield washer antifreeze does in your car….

amphibians: animals that live both on land and in water
employ: use
comfy: comfortable

ice crystals: small pieces of ice with sharp edges
tissues: collection of similar cells, such as muscle or skin

From: Collicutt, Doug. "Some frogs hibernate, some become 'frog-cicles'." *Winnipeg Free Press, Sunday Magazine: What's Outdoors.* (www.naturenorth.com)

IT'S FREEZING!

Frogs put extra sugar in their cells to keep sharp ice crystals from forming. In this activity, you will see how corn syrup—a mixture of a large amount of sugar in a small amount of water—changes the way water freezes.

What You Need:
- corn syrup
- water, room temperature
- 3 small plastic cups
- masking tape
- permanent marker
- measuring spoons
- freezer

What to Do:
1. Put one teaspoon of water in a small cup. Label the cup "water."
2. Put one teaspoon of corn syrup in another small cup. Label it "corn syrup."
3. Put one-half teaspoon of corn syrup into a third cup. Add one-half teaspoon of water and stir the mixture thoroughly. Label it "water and corn syrup."
4. Observe the liquids in the cups and record your observations in the table.
5. Place the cups in the freezer.
6. After a half hour, remove the cups and observe the contents again. Record your observations in the table. If you see any ice crystals, add drawings of them to your observations.

What Do You See?
Record your observations in the data table.

Liquid	Observations Before Freezer	Observations After Freezer
Water		
Corn Syrup		
Water–Corn Syrup Mixture		

ANALYZE THE DATA Review your descriptions of the contents of the three cups that came out of the freezer.

▶ *If any of the cups had ice crystals, describe how the crystals in those cups differed.*

_____

_____

_____

When sugar-water does begin to freeze, the sugar molecules get in the way of the water molecules as they begin to link up to make long ice crystals.

▶ *What evidence did you find that shows this?*

_____

When anything is dissolved in a liquid, the mixture will stay completely liquid at lower temperatures than the pure liquid will. We say that the dissolved substance lowers the freezing point of the liquid.

▶ *How might this be helpful to frogs?*

_____

_____

APPLY KNOWLEDGE Think about some of the foods you might find in your freezer at home. Some items are rock-hard and some are softer.

▶ *Use what you have learned in this activity to explain why ice cubes are hard and brittle while Popsicles are soft enough to bite right through.*

_____

_____

Sorbet is a soft, frozen, ice cream-like dessert made from frozen fruit juice, sugar, and water. There are lots of recipes for homemade sorbet. Suppose your father tried making sorbet one day. You thought it tasted okay but it was too hard, almost like ice.

▶ *How would you suggest your father change the recipe the next time he made a batch of sorbet? How would you explain your suggestion to him?*

_____

_____

_____

It's a Matter of State

Hot Stuff

Is it possible to change the boiling point of water?

As you learned in Lesson 40, sugar can lower the freezing point of water. Can adding sugar to water change the boiling point, too? Normally, water boils when its temperature reaches 100°C. Would sugar-water boil at the same temperature?

▶ **Experiment**

IT'S BOILING!

Test the effect of sugar on the boiling point of water.

What You Need:
- water
- corn syrup
- 2 beakers
- teaspoon
- 100-mL graduated cylinder
- hot plate
- oven mitts
- thermometer
- safety goggles
- watch or clock with seconds

What to Do:
1. Put 100 mL of water into a beaker. Place the beaker on a hot plate.
2. Before you turn on the hot plate, take the temperature of the water, and record it in the data table. Record the time on the same line.
3. Put on the safety goggles. Turn on the hot plate. Take the temperature of the water every two minutes until the water boils. Do not leave the thermometer in the beaker between readings.
4. A liquid has reached its true boiling point when bubbles form within the liquid and break through the surface. Take one more temperature reading two minutes after the water has started to boil. Record your data in the data table. Circle the last temperature. This is the boiling point.
5. Turn off the hot plate. Put on the oven mitts. Carefully move the beaker to a safe place where it can cool.
6. How do you think adding sugar (in the form of corn syrup) to water will affect its boiling point? Write a prediction using an "if/then" statement: IF something happens, THEN something else will happen.

_____

_____

7. Add 3 teaspoons of corn syrup to 100 mL of water in another beaker. Stir the mixture very well. Place the beaker on the hot plate. Repeat steps 2–5.

What Do You See?

Record your temperature data in the charts.

Plain water (100 mL)	
Time (min)	Temperature (°C)

Water (100 mL) and 3 tsp corn syrup	
Time (min)	Temperature (°C)

 Propose Explanations

ANALYZE THE DATA

▶ *How did the boiling point of the corn syrup-water mixture compare to the boiling point of plain water?*

_____

_____

▶ *What can you conclude about the effect of adding sugar on the boiling point of water?*

_____

_____

_____

▶ *Do the results support your hypothesis from Step 6? Explain.*

_____

_____

_____

_____

_____

It's a Matter of State

What a Change!

Flash! Cra-ack! The power of a thunderstorm is amazing!

Have you ever seen a tree that was split in half by a lightning strike? A bolt of lightning carries quite a punch. Scientists at the University of Florida are studying how lightning affects different objects. Martin Uman is part of the research team. He and the team have found fascinating changes in soil that has been struck by lightning.

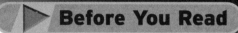 **Before You Read**

THAT'S POWERFUL! You have probably walked across a thick carpet and then felt a shock when you touched a doorknob. That shock is a tiny discharge of electrical energy. A lightning strike is similar, but transfers much more energy. It can also do much more damage than a little shock can.

▶ *Think about thunderstorms you have experienced or seen reported on news programs. List some effects that lightning can have when it strikes things.*

_____

_____

_____

_____

_____

_____

_____

_____

 **Read**

NOTEZONE

Underline the substances in the soil melted by the lightning.
Circle what happens when the soil cools.

What happens when lightning strikes the ground? It keeps on going!

UNDERGROUND LIGHTNING

When researchers from the University of Florida began digging into the ground where a lightning bolt had hit, they thought it would be just another minor excavation.

But the longer they worked, digging along the glassy path left behind by the dirt-melting lightning, the more apparent it became that this was no ordinary dig. What they finally unearthed was verified recently by the Guinness Book of Records as the world's longest fulgurite ever excavated.... The record-breaking fulgurite includes two branches, one almost 16 feet long and the other reaching 17 feet....

Fulgurites have been described by some as solidified lightning bolts. They are glassy tubes that lightning forms below the ground as it tears through the soil. The lightning melts the sand, which solidifies again when it cools to form the hollow glassy material....

"If a normal citizen tries to dig one of these out of the ground," Uman said, "they would destroy it because fulgurites are so fragile. It takes experts who are skilled in working with special tools and are used to digging up fossil bones. It's definitely an art."

....

excavation: digging exploration   **solidified:** made into a solid
verified: showed to be true

From: Meisenheimer, Karen. "Experts From UF Dig Up World's Longest Solidified Lightning Bolt."
University of Florida UF News. (www.napa.ufl.edu/oldnews/fulgur.htm)

FIND OUT MORE

SCIENCE SAURUS

States of Matter   253

SCI LINKS
THE WORLD'S A CLICK AWAY

www.scilinks.org
Keyword: Compounds
Code: GSPD18

READ A DATA TABLE You are familiar with ice melting into water, and you have certainly seen steam rising from boiling water. We do not often think of rocks melting, though, and it is even harder to imagine a rock boiling.

Melting is the change from a solid to a liquid. The melting point of a substance is a characteristic property of the substance. This means that any solid sample melts at that temperature, no matter how large or small the sample is.

The table below lists the melting points of several substances. As you can see, the melting points cover a wide range of temperatures.

Substance	Melting Point (°C)
Aluminum	660
Baking chocolate	36
Copper	1083
Ethylene glycol (antifreeze)	-13
Iron	1535
Mercury	-39
Paraffin (wax)	51
Sodium chloride (salt)	801
Silicon dioxide (sand)	1610
Titanium	1675
Tungsten	3410
Water	0

Room temperature is usually about 20°C.

▶ *Circle the names of substances that are liquid at room temperature.*

▶ *Place a check mark (✓) next to substances that are solid at room temperature, but could be melted in a kitchen oven set to 200°C.*

Lightning itself isn't hot, but everything it passes through is heated to extremely high temperatures.

▶ *According to the chart, how high does lightning have to raise the temperature of sand (silicon dioxide) in order to melt it?*

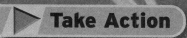

RESEARCH HOW GLASS IS MADE Every day, you use objects made of glass. You look through glass windows. You might drink out of containers made of glass. Some of the cookware in your kitchen may be made of glass. Perhaps someone in your family collects glass figurines. Even the insulation in the walls of your home could contain glass, in the form of fiberglass.

Glass has many uses, and for each use there is a different kind of glass. All glass starts out as sand—silicon dioxide. The silicon dioxide is melted, and chemicals are added to give the glass the properties that are needed. For example, adding borax to the mixture produces the kind of glass used to make the beakers you use in the laboratory. This kind of glass can stand sudden changes in temperature without breaking.

Choose a kind of glass and find out how it is made. Organize what you learn in a display. You might want to make a flowchart that describes the process. You might make drawings that show the ingredients and the product. Choose any way you like to communicate the information you find.

Mixtures, Solutions, and Suspensions

Suspending Snow

Have you ever bought a snow globe as a souvenir?

A snow globe usually shows a scene of a well-known place. It contains a clear liquid and particles suspended within the liquid. You shake the globe, then watch solid particles of white "snow" drift through a clear liquid and fall over the scene. In order to look like real snow, the white particles can't fall too fast or too slow.

 ▶ **Activity**

MAKE A SNOW GLOBE

Figure out what makes the best "snow" by trying different combinations of liquids and solids.

What You Need:
- small jar (such as a baby food jar, instant coffee jar, or jelly jar)
- test tubes with stoppers
- liquids to test (water, baby oil, corn syrup, vegetable oil)
- solids to test (Epsom salts, baking soda, table salt, borax soap)
- measuring spoons

What to Do:
1. Test the first combination in the chart by pouring the liquid into a test tube and adding a small spoonful of the solid. Be sure to stopper the test tube before shaking.
2. Record your observations in the chart.
3. Repeat steps 1 and 2 with other combinations in the chart until you find one that works well. Show your results to your teacher before going on.
4. To make your snow globe, decide how much of each ingredient to use. Add your "winning combination" to the small jar. Make sure the lid is tight before you shake the jar.

What Do You See?

For each combination you try, write your observations in the appropriate box on the chart.

	Water	Corn Syrup	Baby Oil	Vegetable Oil
Borax Soap				
Epsom Salts				
Baking Soda				
Table Salt				

▶ *In your experiment, which mixture of a liquid and a solid looked the most like falling snow? Explain.*

_____

_____

_____

DRAWING CONCLUSIONS Snow globes are an example of a special kind of mixture called a *suspension*. In a suspension, tiny particles are suspended—or hung—within the liquid. The tiny particles in a snow globe are suspended in the liquid for a short time after you shake it.

In a snow globe suspension, the particles are large enough to see clearly. In other suspensions, the particles may not be visible but they are large enough to scatter or block light. This makes the mixture appear cloudy. In any suspension, the particles are heavy enough that they slowly fall and collect on the bottom. They will not remain mixed if they are not stirred or shaken.

▶ *Go back to your results chart. Circle any combination that made a suspension.*

FIND OUT MORE

SCIENCESAURUS

Mixtures, Solutions, and Suspensions 271

Mixtures, Solutions, and Suspensions

Smooth and Creamy

Discover the secret of how a very special treat was first created.

From candy bars to chocolate milk to ice cream toppings, milk chocolate is a favorite treat of many. In the 1860s, Daniel Peter, an ambitious young man in Switzerland, was interested in getting into the chocolate business. To create a unique product, he began experimenting with mixing milk and chocolate to make creamy milk chocolate.

Peter started by simply adding plain milk to chocolate, but that didn't work. His neighbor happened to be Henri Nestlé, a baby food manufacturer. Nestlé was working on a new form of milk. You'll see how Daniel Peter was able to use that product to make milk chocolate.

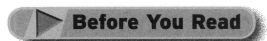 ▶ **Before You Read**

ALL THINGS CHOCOLATE Dark chocolate is a mixture made from cacao seeds, sugar, and flavorings. When you add milk to dark chocolate, you get milk chocolate.

▶ *What foods can you name that contain chocolate?*

_____

_____

▶ *Describe the flavor of milk chocolate.*

_____

_____

▶ *Have you ever had dark chocolate? How does it compare with milk chocolate?*

_____

_____

NOTEZONE

Underline why Daniel Peter's idea of mixing plain milk with dark chocolate did not create creamy chocolate.

Lucky for us, the inventor of milk chocolate candy had a friend, Henri Nestlé, who was an expert on milk.

The Tale of Henri Nestlé and Daniel Peter

...Henri Nestlé...was...an inventive pharmacist and humanitarian. Nestlé wanted to create an alternative to breast milk for mothers who were unable to breast feed their babies.

Infant mortality rates during the 1860s were high due to malnutrition and Henri Nestlé worked hard to battle this widespread problem.... Through his experiments, Henri Nestlé developed a product similar to breast milk that actually saved a child's life. He called this new product Farine Lactée Nestlé.

Around this same time, Daniel Peter, a friend of Henri Nestlé, was trying to successfully mix dark chocolate with milk to create a smooth and creamy chocolate. But his idea was not working because the water present in milk caused the chocolate to separate. He soon combined the dark chocolate with the condensed milk created by Henri Nestlé, and the rest, as they say, is chocolate history. Daniel Peter produced the first milk chocolate bar by adding condensed milk to dark chocolate.

FARINE LACTÉE NESTLÉ

FARINE LACTÉE NESTLÉ
30 ANS DE SUCCÈS

ALIMENT COMPLET POUR LES ENFANTS

Mᵒⁿ HENRI NESTLÉ. A. CHRISTEN. 16. Rue du Parc Royal. PARIS.

---

inventive: creative
pharmacist: a person who prepares medicines
humanitarian: a person who tries to help other people

mortality: death
malnutrition: poor diet
condensed milk: milk with some of the water removed and sugar added

FIND OUT MORE

SCIENCESAURUS
Mixtures, Solutions, and Suspensions 271

From: "The Tale of Henri Nestlé and Daniel Peter." Chocolatevalley.com (www.chocolatevalley.com/history/tale.htm)

MILKY MIXTURES The milk that Daniel Peter first tried to mix with chocolate was plain cow's milk. Cow's milk is about **88** percent water. Fat globules, sugars, and proteins make up the other **12** percent.

The sugar is completely dissolved in the water. You can't see the sugar particles and they will never settle to the bottom.

Tiny fat globules are evenly spread throughout the water. This gives the liquid its creamy white color. But fat molecules always stay separate from water molecules. Since fat is also lighter than water, the fat globules eventually rise. This fat creates a layer of thick cream on the surface of the milk.

Even after the fat has risen to the top, the milk is still whitish in color. This comes from the protein particles that are still spread throughout the water. These protein particles will never settle out, but they are big enough to reflect light. This is why even skim milk, which has no fat globules, is not clear.

The chart below describes three types of mixtures. Complete the chart by writing what components of milk form each type of mixture.

Mixture Type	Properties	Milk Components
Solution	particles are invisible, do not separate	
Colloid	particles do not separate but are big enough to reflect light	
Suspension	particles separate out	

Condensed milk has had about half of the water removed while all the other substances remain. Then extra sugar is added.

▶ *Is condensed milk a colloid, suspension, or solution? Explain your answer.*

_____

_____

▶ *Why do you think condensed milk mixes better with chocolate than whole milk does? (If you need to, look back at the reading.)*

_____

_____

_____

A RECIPE FOR DISASTER

Here's a recipe for smooth chocolate milk—or is it?

What You Need:

- melted dark chocolate (baking chocolate)
- 2 dishes or bowls
- 2 spoons or stirrers
- whole milk at room temperature
- condensed milk at room temperature
- masking tape
- marking pen

What to Do:

1. Label one bowl "whole" and the other "condensed."
2. Put some melted dark chocolate in the bowl marked "whole."
3. Add about the same amount of whole milk.
4. Stir to mix well.
5. Record your observations in the table.
6. Pour some melted chocolate into the bowl marked "condensed."
7. Add an equal amount of condensed milk and stir.
8. Record your observations in the table.

Milk Product Added	Observations
Whole milk	
Condensed milk	

What Do You See?

▶ *What does the mixture in the cup with whole milk look like?*

_____

_____

▶ *Describe why Daniel Peter might have found this result unsatisfactory.*

_____

▶ *What did Daniel Peter conclude caused the problem when he tried mixing milk and melted chocolate like this?*

_____

▶ *What did you observe with the condensed milk that supports Daniel Peter's conclusion?*

_____

_____

161

Mixtures, Solutions, and Suspensions

SODA POP SCIENCE

What puts the *pop* in soda pop?

Old, stale soda pop—blah. It still has the same flavor, but it just doesn't taste as good as a freshly opened bottle. Why? What makes a fresh soda pop different? If you look at the ingredients on a bottle of soda pop, you will notice that one of the many things it contains is "carbonated water." That is just plain water with carbon dioxide gas dissolved in it. But it is this dissolved carbon dioxide that gives fresh soda its sharp, tangy taste. What do you think happens to make a soda pop go flat?

 ▶ **Before You Read**

GASSY LIQUIDS Imagine you come home from school, open the refrigerator, and take out a can of soda pop.

▶ *What do you see on the surface of the soda pop right after it is poured into a glass?*

_____

_____

▶ *What happens after the soda has been open for a long time?*

_____

_____

People who make soda pop want to keep it fizzy until you drink it.

▶ *Do you know what they do to keep the bubbles dissolved in the liquid? Write any ideas you have.*

_____

_____

NOTEZONE

Underline the gas that is dissolved in soda pop.

Circle what happens to the gas when you open a bottle of soda pop.

Here's how the gas gets into the soda pop and (usually) stays there.

The Fizz Factor

Rarely do you ever drink an entire 2-liter bottle of soda at one sitting. Since leftovers are inevitable, the soda tends to go flat....

Since the fizz in the soda is actually dissolved carbon dioxide gas, the goal is to keep as much of the gas in the bottle as possible. Soda fizzes when dissolved carbon dioxide gas is released in the form of bubbles. At the bottling plant, carbon dioxide molecules are forced into the soda in an amount that is greater than would ordinarily dissolve.... As soon as you open the bottle, ... excess gas escapes into the room...

The higher the gas pressure above the liquid in the bottle, the more gas will be pressed into the liquid. Makes sense. However, here's the kicker. Once you open the bottle, ... carbon dioxide molecules that were forced into the soda at the bottling plant come flying out. It's that unmistakable sound of PSSSSST!

---

inevitable: unavoidable
dissolved: completely mixed in and no longer visible
excess: extra

From: Wolke, Robert L. *What Einstein Didn't Know: Scientific Answers to Everyday Questions.* Delacorte Press.

DIAGRAM SOLUTIONS   Soda pop is a solution. In a solution, one substance (called the solute) is dissolved in another substance (called the solvent). In many cases, the solute is a powder (a solid) and the solvent is a liquid.

► *Can you think of a familiar example of such a solution?*

_____

But not all solutions are made up of solids dissolved in liquids.

► *What is the solute in soda pop? What is the solvent?*

_____

Look at the diagram of three bottles of soda pop. Bottle 1 is unopened, Bottle 2 has just been opened, and Bottle 3 has been open for several hours. Use arrows to show what is happening to the carbon dioxide in each bottle. Beneath each bottle, write a brief description of what is happening in the bottle. Use some of the following terms in your labels or descriptions: *carbon dioxide gas (CO$_2$)*, *dissolved carbon dioxide gas*, *in solution*, *out of solution*, *pressure*. Use the reading as needed to help you label each diagram.

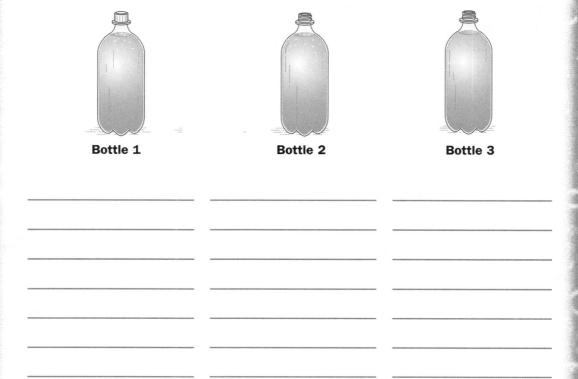

Bottle 1   **Bottle 2**   **Bottle 3**

CARBONATED CANDY Have you ever tasted the candy that sizzles and fizzles in your mouth? The manufacturer makes it by forcing carbon dioxide gas under high pressure into a hot liquid sugar mixture. When the mixture cools and hardens, tiny pressurized bubbles of carbon dioxide gas are trapped within the hard candy.

► *How is making this candy similar to making soda pop?*

_____

_____

_____

What happens when you put the candy on your tongue? First, it begins to dissolve in the water in your saliva—like other candies. Then, your tongue starts to tingle and you hear popping sounds.

► *What do you think makes your tongue tingle? What causes the popping sounds? (Think about what you hear when you open a can of soda and what your tongue feels when you drink it.)*

_____

_____

_____

_____

_____

► *How is eating a piece of carbonated candy similar to opening a can of soda pop?*

_____

_____

_____

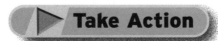

► Take Action

INVENT A NEW TREAT Use your imagination to invent a new food product that uses carbon dioxide to add fizz. On a separate sheet of paper, explain how the food product would be manufactured or packaged to keep the carbon dioxide trapped. Then create an advertisement to describe this new treat.

Properties of Elements

The Nifty 92

What are you made of?

How many ingredients do you think it would take to build every different thing in the world?

 **Read**

NOTEZONE

Underline the names of elements mentioned in the reading.

(Circle) the adjectives that describe them.

Newspaper writer Kathy Wollard called the 92 naturally occurring elements the "Nifty 92."

The Nifty 92

...The ancient Greeks thought that everything in the world was made of four basic elements: water, fire, earth, and air. You, your dog, and your banana split were simply combinations of the Big Four....

Everything is indeed made of elements....[T]here are 92 natural elements that make everything you see around you. The Nifty 92 are the ingredients in the recipes for cats and clouds, bats and belfries.

(There also are a handful of man-made elements, concocted in laboratories; rather rickety as elements go.)

Many of the Nifty 92 are utterly familiar: good old oxygen. Shiny copper and silver. Slippery mercury. Balloon-lifting helium. Bone-building calcium. Poisonous arsenic. Radiant neon. Others are unfamiliar, tongue-twisting oddballs: Lanthanum. Scandium. Cerium. Praseodymium. Yttrium.

Scientists use a big chart called the Periodic Table that shows all the elements, starting with hydrogen. Why does first place go to hydrogen? Hydrogen is the simplest element....

...[S]tarting with atoms of the Nifty 92, combined in myriad molecules, a whole universe is built, from chocolate-chip cookies to soaring mountains to you and me.

belfries: bell towers
concocted: made
rickety: shaky, unstable
utterly: very

atoms: the smallest parts of elements
myriad: very, very many
molecules: combinations of atoms

From: Wollard, Kathy. "Atoms Like To Stick Together." *Newsday.*

FIND OUT MORE

SCIENCESAURUS

Properties of Matter	251
Atoms	255
Elements	260
Periodic Table	265

SCILINKS.
THE WORLD'S A CLICK AWAY

www.scilinks.org
Keyword: Periodic Table
Code: GSPD20

▶ Explore

PERIODIC TABLE OF THE ELEMENTS Look at a copy of the periodic table. You can find one in a reference book such as *ScienceSaurus* or an encyclopedia. You can also find one on the Internet.

▶ *Locate the "Nifty 92" (elements 1–92). What element is number 92?*

_____

The number 92 stands for the atomic number, which is the number of protons in the nucleus of a uranium atom. Look at the box for element 92 again.

▶ *What other information about uranium is there?*

_____

_____

_____

▶ *What is the name of the first "rickety" element? (Hint: They start with element 93.)*

_____

▶ *Look at the Nifty 92 as a group. Now look at the "rickety" elements as a group. How do their atomic masses compare?*

_____

▶ *What conclusion can you draw about the relationship between atomic mass and stability?*

_____

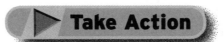

▶ Take Action

WRITE EXPRESSIVELY Kathy Wollard uses adjectives to describe how some of the elements look, or what they do.

Do research to find out more about the elements below. Then write your own adjective to describe each one in the blank space beside its name.

Aluminum	Zinc
Gold	Iron
Lead	Carbon
Tin	Radium
Iodine	Platinum

Properties of Elements

Smelly Sulfur

▲ "Snottites"

How can you tell what elements are around you?

Sometimes you can smell the chlorine from a swimming pool before you can even see the pool. The odor of ammonia in window cleaners makes you wrinkle your nose before you notice the bottle. The sulfur smell of one little rotten egg can fill a whole room. Some elements and compounds have properties that are so distinct, your nose can identify them from a distance.

Molecules of chlorine, ammonia, or hydrogen sulfide gases float through the air into your nose. As your nose senses these molecules, it sends a message to your brain, which identifies the smell. With just a sniff and a little knowledge of chemistry, you can actually name many of the elements and compounds in your surroundings. And some day this ability could save your life!

▶ **Before You Read**

CAVE CONDITIONS Have you ever been in a cave? Have you read about caves or seen a movie or television show about caves? What would you expect to see, hear, and smell in a cave?

_____

_____

_____

_____

_____

_____

_____

_____

▶ Read

Here's how *National Geographic* writer John L. Eliot describes Villa Luz, a cave in Mexico that he and some scientists explored.

DEADLY HAVEN

We could smell the cave long before we saw it. Along the mile-and-a-half (2.4-kilometer) trail from the Almandro River a natural paradise unfolded. Oropendolas, hummingbirds, motmots, and other tropical birds perched in ceiba and quebracho trees. Leafcutter ants paraded across our path in this lush rain forest in southern Mexico's Tabasco state. But as the rotten-egg stench increased, paradise was about to be lost. At the entrance of the cave my scientific companions—all accomplished cavers—and I donned respirators for protection against the vapors within.

Then we descended. Louise Hose, a geologist at California's Chapman University, led me to a rock wall...[covered] with long white mucus-like colonies of sulfur-eating bacteria.

"We joke that this cave has a cold, and we call these 'snottites'," Hose said. The bacteria oxidize sulfur compounds in subterranean springs that feed into the cave. Sulfur is the basis for nearly all [the cave's]...life.

---

paradise: a place of great beauty
stench: a strong, bad odor
donned: put on
respirators: gas masks

vapors: gases
mucus-like: dripping, gooey
oxidize: combine with oxygen
subterranean: below ground

From: Eliot, John L. "Deadly Haven." *National Geographic.* (www.nationalgeographic.com/ngm/0105/feature4)

Underline why the explorers had to wear respirators.

Circle the words used to describe the gases in the cave.

FIND OUT MORE

SCIENCESAURUS

Properties of Matter	251
Elements, Molecules, and Compounds	259
Chemical Formulas	267

SCI LINKS
THE WORLD'S A CLICK AWAY

www.scilinks.org
Keyword: Elements
Code: GSPD21

WHAT'S THAT SMELL? When bacteria take sulfur (S) from the rocks and combine it with hydrogen (H), they make hydrogen sulfide (H_2S). Hydrogen sulfide is the stinky gas that John Eliot and the scientists smelled as they approached the cave.

$$S + 2H \rightarrow H_2S$$

Then other bacteria combine some of the H_2S with oxygen (O_2) that enters the cave from outside. H_2S and O_2 make sulfuric acid (H_2SO_4). Sulfuric acid is a powerful acid that can slowly dissolve rock.

$$H_2S + 2O_2 \rightarrow H_2SO_4$$

Use this information to create a graphic organizer. Add action verbs and arrows to the diagram below to show how the bacteria start the process that dissolves rock. Be sure to include the terms *bacteria*, *hydrogen sulfide (H_2S)*, *oxygen (O_2)*, *sulfuric acid (H_2SO_4)*, and *rock* in the diagram.

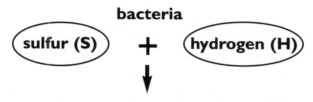

MAKE INFERENCES You know that the acid produced by these sulfur-eating bacteria can slowly dissolve rock.

▶ *Imagine a small cave that had formed in a giant rock. Describe what could happen if sulfuric acid dripped in that cave for millions of years.*

_____

_____

Go back to your graphic organizer. Add one more step that shows how a cave is formed as rock dissolves.

▶ Propose Explanations

SHOULD WE KEEP GOING? The "rotten-egg stench" is caused by the gas hydrogen sulfide (H_2S). High concentrations of H_2S can damage a person's lungs. Extremely high concentrations can make a person pass out and even die. The gas has a strong odor at first. But after a short while a person gets used to it and can no longer smell it.

▶ *Look at the respirator worn by geologist Louise Hose on the right. Why do you think she is wearing it over her mouth and nose?*

_____

_____

_____

_____

_____

_____

▶ *The explorers wear gas monitors that tell when hydrogen sulfide is present. Why is it important that the scientists wear gas monitors?*

_____

_____

_____

_____

▶ *Look at the picture of Louise Hose again. What other pieces of safety equipment can you see? Why do you think they are used?*

_____

_____

_____

_____

Properties of Elements

Silicon Creature

The periodic table gives us information about 100+ elements.

Which element in the periodic table is most important to you? Gold? Silver? What about carbon—the element that diamonds are made from? In fact, diamonds are pretty, but plain old carbon is truly precious.

In fact, there is an entire branch of chemistry (called organic chemistry) that involves only molecules that contain carbon atoms with hydrogens hooked on (and a few other atoms here and there). Organic chemistry is important because all living things are made up of these carbon-based molecules.

▶ **Before You Read**

SCIENCE FICTION Science-fiction writers begin with actual science facts. Then they play with the ideas and write about what they imagine could be different. In the television show *Star Trek,* Captain Kirk and his crew on the starship *Enterprise* explored "strange new worlds" in outer space. Outer space exists, but the fascinating creatures the crew met and the interesting cultures they visited do not.

▶ *What makes science fiction valuable? What value might there be in imagining things beyond those that we know really exist?*

_____

_____

_____

_____

_____

_____

_____

_____

_____

 **Read**

NOTEZONE

Underline why carbon is special for life.

Neal Meglathery hosts a radio show from a science museum in Vermont. Here he explains why carbon is something we cannot live without.

Carbon and Silicon

Hi this is Neal, and I'm here to talk to you about...you know...the little talk that we need to have at some point in our lives. THE talk. About life. The birds, the bees. So please bear with me. What I'm trying to say is, life as we know it...is based on...carbon. The sixth element in the periodic table. Oh, the other elements are important, all right. Where would we be without hydrogen, or helium, or oxygen? We wouldn't be here having this discussion, I can tell you that! But carbon is special because...[a]bout 24 percent of your body is made up of carbon. So carbon is more than just cheap pencil lead. Carbon makes all life possible.

In an old episode of Star Trek, Captain Kirk and his [brave]...crew stumble across a mining operation where solid, round nodes are being dug up. The miners think these things are inert lumps of silicon but...they turn out to be the eggs of a very displeased creature. ...[T]he Enterprise crew was surprised to find a life form that appeared to be silicon-based. See, we refer to all life forms here on earth as "carbon-based." Carbon is important because it has the ability to form four separate bonds with other atoms. That means a carbon atom can share four of its six electrons with other atoms. Oxygen can make only two bonds and hydrogen only one. So carbon is a bonding champ.

▲ The *Enterprise* crew

FIND OUT MORE

SCIENCESAURUS
DNA   115
Properties
  of Matter   251
Atoms   255
Elements, Molecules,
  and Compounds 259
Periodic Table   265
Chemical
  Formulas   267

www.scilinks.org
Keyword: Elements
Code: GSPD21

nodes: clumps
inert: not moving
bonds: connections

electrons: negatively charged particles that surround the core (or nucleus) of an atom

From: Meglathery, Neal. "Montshire Minute: Carbon." *The Montshire Minute.* Montshire Museum of Science. (www.montshire.net/minute/mm011126.html)

WHAT THE TABLE SHOWS Here is one column from the periodic table of the elements. This column is called the "carbon group." Each square contains the chemical symbol of one element. Each element's atomic number, at the top of the square, tells how many protons the atom has in its nucleus. Below the element name is the number called the atomic mass. That is the average mass of an atom of that element.

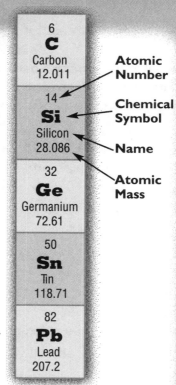

Elements are arranged in the table so that all the elements in one column have the same number of electrons in the outermost electron cloud of their atoms. The number of electrons in the outermost electron cloud determines how an atom interacts with other atoms. That means all atoms in one column react to other atoms in similar ways.

You learned in the reading that carbon can share four of its electrons with other atoms. This means it has four electrons in its outermost electron cloud.

▶ *What can you infer about the number of electrons in the outermost electron cloud of a silicon atom based on silicon's position on the periodic table?*

_____

_____

▶ *What can you infer about how silicon might bond with other atoms to form molecules?*

_____

_____

A science-fiction writer combines scientific facts with imagination to create stories that are at least somewhat believable.

▶ *Why do you think the writers of* Star Trek *chose to base their imaginary life form on the element silicon?*

_____

_____

_____

_____

_____

Propose Explanations

WHY NOT SILICON? Neal Meglathery said that carbon makes all life possible. Silicon is very similar to carbon in some ways, but small differences turn out to matter a lot.

Atoms with higher atomic numbers have more protons, neutrons, and electrons. They are bigger, so they have to "stretch" more to bond with each other. This usually makes the bond weaker.

▶ *How does silicon's atomic number compare to carbon's?*

_____

▶ *What can you infer about the strength of a silicon-silicon bond compared to a carbon-carbon bond?*

_____

Many molecules in the bodies of plants and animals are very long and complex. DNA is one example. This "molecule of life" is built from millions of carbon atoms bonded together.

▶ *Given what you know about silicon-silicon bonds, what can you infer about the likelihood that silicon-based life could exist?*

_____

_____

_____

Take Action

WRITE A REVIEW In the *Star Trek* episode, the crew discovers a life form that is apparently silicon-based and lives in a cave.

▶ *Write a review that discusses the science of this episode. What parts of the episode were based on scientific facts? Which were imagined or made up? Why is it interesting to consider the silicon question?*

_____

_____

_____

_____

_____

_____

_____

UNIT 5
Interactions of Matter

Matter is interacting all around you all the time. Can you feel it? When matter interacts with other matter, neat things happen. If the interaction is chemical, new substances are produced. Sometimes heat is given off, or light, or noise. But if you've ever marveled at the wonders of Velcro, you know that physical interactions of matter are just as interesting.

In this unit you'll take a look at some of the different ways matter interacts with other matter. You'll identify the chemical reactions that make a cake rise. You'll find out what makes Jell-O jiggle and how snakes use venom to disarm their prey. You'll see how chemicals can be mixed to make light, and how scientists experiment to make "super" materials in the laboratory.

? Did You Know?

Velcro was invented by a guy who noticed the burrs that were sticking so well to his socks after a hike. Examining them under a microscope, he saw that the hooks of the burrs fit perfectly into the loops of the fabric that made up his socks.

Chemical Bonds

Unnaturally Curly Hair

Is your hair curly or straight?

Hair is one of the first things we mention when we are describing a person. There are so many varieties of hair shape—straight, wavy, curly, frizzy, and everything in between. But many people do all kinds of things to change the hair they're born with.

You might be surprised to know that the main substance that makes up hair is the same in everyone. But small differences in the chemical bonds within strands cause big differences in shape and texture.

▲ **Curlers give straight hair a different shape**

▶ Before You Read

CHANGING HAIR Do you ever do anything to your hair to make it look different? Lots of people do. If you've ever looked at the hair-care aisle of the drug store, you know there are lots of products you can use.

▶ *Think of the ways you and your friends try to change your hair shape. What products or tools do you use?*

_____

_____

_____

_____

_____

▶ Read

Read about the chemical bonds that make your hair curl.

A "Permanent" Change

When you curl your hair—whether it's with water and styling gel or a permanent-wave kit—you are messing with the chemical bonds that keep the protein fibers of your hair's cortex stuck together. These chemical bonds include hydrogen bonds [and disulfide bonds]....

When you wet your hair, water molecules sneak in between the proteins of the cortex and [break the] hydrogen bonds.... If you set your wet hair in curlers or pull your curly hair straight, then let it dry in this new shape, the hydrogen bonds will reform in a new position. Of course, when your hair gets wet again, those hydrogen bonds will weaken and then reform in their original position, giving you back the hair you didn't want—making curly hair straight, straight hair curly.

If you want a permanent change, you can perm your hair. In a perm, you don't just break hydrogen bonds, you also break the disulfide bonds that hold the proteins together. You add chemicals that break the disulfide bonds (bonds between sulfur atoms). Then you reshape your hair and add chemicals that reconstruct those disulfide bonds, holding your hair in a new shape. Since these disulfide bonds withstand water, your new hairdo will be waterproof.

protein: type of molecule found in the body
cortex: the body of a hair

From: "Better Hair Through Chemistry: It's Enough to Curl Your Hair." *Exploring Online.* The Exploratorium. (www.exploratorium.edu/exploring/hair/hair_4.html)

FIND OUT MORE

SCIENCESAURUS
Cell Processes   079
Elements, Molecules,
  and Compounds   259
Chemical Bonds   263

SCILINKS.
THE WORLD'S A CLICK AWAY

Keyword: Types of
Chemical Bonds
Code: GSPD22

ORGANIZING INFORMATION The reading describes two different processes you can use to curl your hair—setting wet hair in curlers and getting a permanent wave.

▶ *Draw a concept map to show what happens to the different bonds in hair when it gets curled by each of the two different processes. Use terms like* hair, water, chemicals, bonds, break, reshape, dry, *and* reform *in your map. Use symbols like arrows and "+" signs to show the relationships between the parts of the map. The map should finish with the term Curly Hair.*

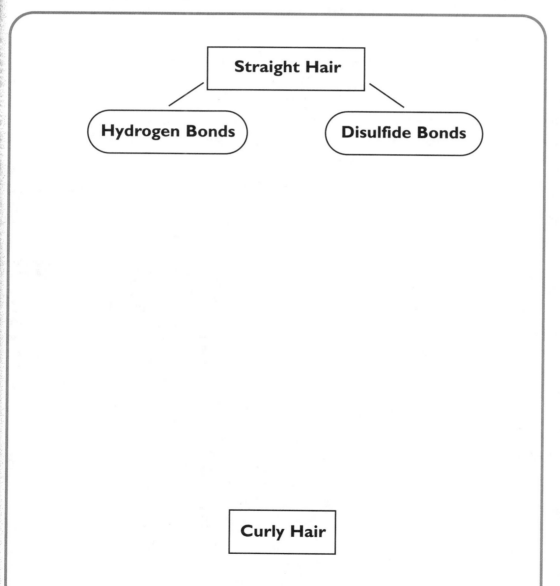

▶ Propose Explanations

HOW PERMANENT? The type of hair you have is determined by your genes. Genes are your body's instructions for how to develop all the parts that make you *you*. Genes control your hair shape by determining how the proteins in your hair will be arranged and which bonds will form between them. Copies of your genes can be found in every cell of your body. In general, things you do to your body do not change your genes.

Let's say that your friend Maya does not like her straight hair. She decides to get a permanent wave. The next day her hair is very curly.

▶ *How will Maya's hair look two years from now if she doesn't have another permanent? Explain in terms of Maya's genes.*

_____

_____

WET SET When your hair is wet, it can be molded into practically any shape because the hydrogen bonds between the protein fibers are broken. As hair begins to dry, water molecules between the fibers evaporate away. Hydrogen bonds then reform between the protein fibers. When it's all dry, the hair has a new shape.

▶ *Use this information to explain how hair brushes and blow-dryers can be used to style hair.*

_____

_____

_____

▶ Take Action

COMPARE AND CONTRAST Draw a Venn diagram to compare two methods of hair-styling: permanent wave and blow-drying.

▶ *What do the two methods have in common? How do they differ?*

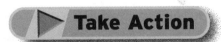

Permanent Wave   Blow-drying

Chemical Bonds

JELL-O JIGGLE

It wiggles, it jiggles, and it's sweet. What is it?

If you've ever eaten in a cafeteria, you have probably eaten a gelatin dessert. What's in it? The key ingredient is gelatin, a colorless substance made of protein. That's what gives a gelatin dessert its jiggle. What about the rest of the dessert? The sweet taste comes from sugar or artificial sweeteners, and artificial colors are added to make it look appetizing. The fruit flavor comes from natural or artificial flavors.

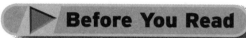 **Before You Read**

SOLID OR LIQUID?

▶ *Have you ever made a gelatin dessert before? What steps did you follow? Write down what you can remember.*

_____

_____

_____

_____

▶ *How would you describe gelatin dessert? Would you call it a solid? A liquid? Can you pick it up? Can you drink it through a straw? Write your ideas about what gelatin is below.*

_____

_____

_____

_____

_____

_____

_____

Underline the two stages of gelatin preparation.

A food scientist describes what makes Jell-O, a gelatin dessert, jiggle.

How does [Jell-O] work?

...When you buy a box of Jell-O (or another brand of gelatin) at the grocery store, you get a small packet of powdered gelatin with artificial flavorings and colors. At room temperature, the gelatin protein is in the form of a triple helix—three separate...polypeptide chains [that] have lined up and twisted around each other.

▲ Powdered gelatin

What happens to gelatin when you add boiling water? The energy of the heated water is enough to break up the weak bonds holding the gelatin strands together. The helical structure falls apart, and you are left with free polypeptide chains floating about in solution.

The next step is to add cold water and stick the dissolved gelatin in the refrigerator to chill for several hours. When you cool down the mixture, the polypeptide chains begin to [bond again] and reform the tight triple helix structure. However, ...the individual strands have been widely dispersed by mixing, so the helices aren't perfectly formed. In some places, there are gaps in the helix, and in others, there is just a tangled web of polypeptide chains. ...[W]ater is trapped inside these gaps and pockets between chains. The protein net that is left after chilling gives the gelatin mold its shape, and the trapped water provides the characteristic Jell-O jiggle....

helix: spiral
polypeptide chain: a smaller piece of a protein

helical: shaped like a spiral
dispersed: spread out

From: "What Exactly Is Jell-O Made From? How Does It Work?" *HowStuff Works.* (www.howstuffworks.com/question557.htm)

FIND OUT MORE

SCIENCESAURUS
Cell Processes   079
Elements, Molecules,
  and Compounds 259
Chemical Bonds   263

SCiLINKS.
THE WORLD'S A CLICK AWAY

www.scilinks.org
Keyword: Types of
  Chemical Bonds
Code: GSPD22

MAKING A GELATIN DESSERT

What You Need:
- three 250-mL beakers, calibrated
- glass-marking pencil
- package of gelatin dessert
- cold water
- boiling water
- stirring rod or spoon
- oven mitt or pot holders
- measuring spoon (tsp.)

What to Do:
1. Number three 250-mL beakers *1*, *2*, and *3*. Mark them with your initials.
2. Put 1 teaspoon of gelatin powder into each of the three beakers.
3. Add 50 mL of cold water to beaker 1 and stir. Ask your teacher to add 50 mL of boiling water to beaker 2 and to beaker 3. Stir.
4. Now add 50 mL of cold water to beaker 1 and to beaker 2 and stir.
5. Ask your teacher to add 50 mL of boiling water to beaker 3. Stir.
6. Put the three beakers into a refrigerator for about 30 minutes.
7. Remove the beakers from the refrigerator and examine the contents. Try shaking the beakers to see if the gelatin jiggles. Try to stir the gelatin or pick up some on a spoon. *Do not taste any of the samples.*

What Did You See?
Record your observations in the table.

Beaker	First Water Added (Hot or Cold?)	Second Water Added (Hot or Cold?)	Appearance of Mixture
1			
2			
3			

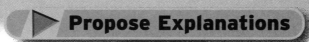
HOLDING IT TOGETHER

Create a graphic organizer to show what happens to the bonds in gelatin during the two stages of preparation described in the reading.

Now review your observations from the activity. Use your graphic organizer to explain what was happening to the gelatin bonds in each beaker during the same two stages of preparation.

Beaker	First Water Added	Second Water Added/Refrigeration
1		
2		
3		

▶ *When making gelatin dessert, what important step must you do when you add the first water?*

_____

_____

_____

▶ *Why does the gelatin dessert recipe tell you to add cold water instead of hot water before putting the gelatin in the refrigerator?*

_____

_____

_____

Chemical Bonds

BENDING STEEL

Steel is specially designed to be strong. But if you get it hot enough, you can hammer it into a new shape.

In Gary Paulsen's novel, *Popcorn Days & Buttermilk Nights*, a 14-year old boy from the city is sent to live with his uncle in farm country after getting into some trouble at home. Uncle David has a blacksmith shop. The boy, Carley, becomes his assistant for the summer. He learns how steel is made into horseshoes, farming tools, and other objects.

The atoms that make up metals are held together by metallic bonds—one type of chemical bond. These bonds allow metals to be hammered into different shapes and give them their other characteristic properties.

NOTEZONE

Underline all the words that give evidence of how hot the forge was.

▶ **Read**

Uncle David gets the idea to create a merry-go-round and Ferris wheel. Carley recalls how he and David became involved in their task.

I Was Coal, I Was Fire

David started as a smithy who was working to build something he needed—a circus for his kids. And I started as a helper. But then everything changed.

I thought we had worked hard before—I didn't know what work was, had no idea. The heat from the forge cooked my face into blisters, peeled the blisters, and then recooked it into more blisters. The process repeated itself until I was leather, until my skin matched my leather sweatband. I was coal, I was fire, I was heat and movement and the *crang CRANG* of hammer to metal and the shower of sparks—I was all of these things just in the first two days and I became a deeper part of them in the following days.

David became steel and smoke and the hammer. When I think of him now, I see him as a flash of white teeth smiling through the burned black of his face and the shower of sparks and the hammer raising and coming down and the steel bending.

forge: fire over which a blacksmith heats metal

From: Paulsen, Gary. *Popcorn Days & Buttermilk Nights*. Puffin Paperback Books.

FIND OUT MORE

SCIENCESAURUS

Elements, Molecules, and Compounds 259
Chemical Bonds 263

▶ Explore

WORKING METAL If you were to pound a solid rock with a hammer, little bits of the rock would break off. Unlike most solids, metals bend instead of breaking when hammered. To help us understand why, let's take a look at the atoms that make up metals.

Look at the diagram of a piece of metal. The "plus" signs represent atoms that make up the metal. These atoms have given up one of their electrons, which are negatively charged. This leaves the atoms positively charged. Charged atoms are known as ions. You can see the negatively charged electrons floating around the ions. Bonds between the positively charged ions and the negatively charged electrons are what hold the metal together. These are called metallic bonds.

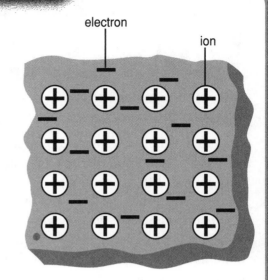

▲ **A piece of metal**

Because the electrons are free to move around the ions, metallic bonds are very flexible. When a piece of metal is hammered, the ions on that side are pushed closer together. In many solids, this would cause the material to break. But because the electrons in metal are free to move around, they can move between the ions in their new positions, and so prevent the material from breaking.

▶ *What did Uncle David and Carley do to the steel before they used hammers to shape it?*

_____

_____

Heat is a form of energy. When you heat metal, you add energy to the atoms that make it up. The added energy causes the atoms to move around more, making the solid less rigid.

▶ *Why do you suppose David and Carley heated the steel before hammering it?*

_____

_____

_____

Reactions in Action

BATTER UP!

Do you like to cook? If you do, you might be a budding chemist.

It's fun to see how a mixture of ingredients can change as it cooks. The cake that you take out of the oven is very different from the gloppy batter that you started with. Is it just the heat from the oven, or does something else happen to cause the changes?

In many ways, a kitchen is like a chemistry lab. You combine foods to produce a tasty dish, just as a chemist combines chemicals. As your dish cooks, it goes through changes. Some of these changes are chemical reactions.

▶ Before You Read

EVERYDAY SCIENCE Even if you haven't done much cooking, you've probably watched someone cook. Think about something you've cooked or watched someone cook. It can be as simple as scrambled eggs, toast, or slice-and-bake cookies.

▶ *Think about the ways in which the food changed as it was cooked. Describe these changes.*

_____

_____

_____

_____

_____

_____

_____

_____

_____

► **Read**

NoteZone

In the directions, underline the steps that seem to be the most important to do correctly.

This cake can be prepared in just a few minutes, but the baker still has to follow directions carefully.

IRVING PRAGER'S CHOCOLATE DUMP CAKE

- 1 cup sugar
- $1\frac{1}{2}$ cups flour
- $\frac{1}{3}$ cup cocoa powder
- 1 tsp baking soda
- 2 tbsp vinegar

- $\frac{1}{2}$ tsp salt
- 2 tsp vanilla
- $\frac{1}{2}$ cup corn oil
- 1 cup cold water

Other equipment: 8-inch cake pan [buttered and floured], fork or wire [whisk], mixing bowl

Preheat oven to 375°F. Be sure the oven is at 375°F before you start to mix the ingredients. With a fork or wire [whisk], mix everything together except the vinegar. Blend well. Add the vinegar, stir quickly, [pour into pan,] and put in the oven as fast as you can.

Bake at 375°F for 20 to 25 minutes until slightly puffed in the middle. Dust with confectioner's sugar. Or melt semi-sweet chocolate chips with a pinch of salt, add several tablespoons of sour cream, mix, and spread on the cake.

ingredients: the foods that are mixed together in a cooking recipe
confectioner's sugar: powdered sugar

From: "Irving Prager's Chocolate Dump Cake." Carnegie Mellon University. (www.cs.cmu.edu/People/rapidproto/activities/food/dumpcake.html)

FIND OUT MORE

SCIENCESAURUS

Chemical Reactions   269

SCiLINKS
THE WORLD'S A CLICK AWAY

www.scilinks.org
Keyword: Chemical Reactions
Code: GSPD23

BUBBLE, BUBBLE

You have probably seen the fizz from the chemical reaction between vinegar and baking soda many times. The "fizz" is what makes the cake rise. Could other liquids be used in place of the vinegar?

What You Need:
- clear plastic cups (small)
- marking pen
- baking soda
- water
- white vinegar
- various liquids used in cooking (corn oil, milk, buttermilk, lemon juice, orange juice, etc.)
- teaspoons
- safety goggles

What to Do:
1. Choose several liquids to test with baking soda. Be sure to include vinegar and water. Show your list to your teacher before you carry out your experiment.
2. After your teacher has approved your list, obtain a cup for each liquid you will test. Label each cup with the name of one of the liquids.
3. Put on your safety goggles. Put about a teaspoon of baking soda into each cup.
4. Add a few teaspoons of water to the cup marked "water" and stir the mixture. Record your observations.
5. Use a clean spoon and repeat step 4 using vinegar and the cup marked "vinegar." Record your observations.
6. Repeat step 5 with the remaining liquids.

Liquid Tested	Observations
Water	
Vinegar	

WHAT DO YOU SEE?

▶ *Which liquids produced a visible reaction with baking soda?*

_____

▶ *What evidence of a chemical reaction did you see?*

_____

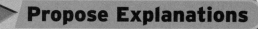

HOW DOES IT WORK? Baking soda is sodium bicarbonate, a chemical that reacts with acids. Vinegar contains acetic acid, so when you mix it with baking soda you get a chemical reaction. Actually, you get two reactions, because the product of the reaction between the sodium bicarbonate and acid breaks down very quickly. Here are the two reactions.

sodium bicarbonate + acetic acid ⟶ carbonic acid

carbonic acid ⟶ carbon dioxide gas + water

▶ *Think about the kinds of liquids that caused a reaction with baking soda. What do these liquids have in common?*

_____

_____

_____

_____

The bubbles you saw in the activity were bubbles of carbon dioxide gas escaping from the mixture. Bubbles trapped in the cake batter make the batter rise slightly before the cake is put into the oven. Inside the oven, heat causes the bubbles to expand, making the cake rise even more.

▶ *Notice that the recipe says to put the batter into the pan and get the pan into the oven as quickly as possible. Why do you think it's important to act so quickly when making this cake?*

_____

_____

_____

_____

▶ *Think back to the differences in the liquids you tested in the activity. How is cake batter different from the mixture of vinegar and baking soda you made in the activity? How might this difference help make the cake rise?*

_____

_____

_____

_____

Reactions in Action

DEADLY VENOM

Are you afraid of snakes?

Imagine that you are hiking along a trail with a friend. It's a sunny day, and you and your friend are enjoying the fresh air and exercise. Suddenly, your friend stops walking and points to the path ahead. A snake! It's right there, just a few yards away from you. What do you think the snake will do next? What should you do?

The venom that snakes inject into their prey is a mixture of powerful chemicals. All the workings of an animal's body, including blood cells, muscle cells, and nerve cells, depend on exactly the right chemicals being in the right place at the right moment. The snake's venom changes all that.

Mojave rattlesnake ▶

▶ Before You Read

SNAKE CHARMS Many people are afraid of snakes, especially people who know very little about them. How much do you know about snakes? Take this little quiz. Mark the statements that you think are true with a *T*. Mark the statements that you think are false with an *F*.

As you read the rest of this lesson, you'll discover the answers. Remember to go back and check your answers to the quiz. Ready? Then try it!

_____ Most species of snakes are venomous (poisonous).

_____ A bite from a nonpoisonous snake is harmless.

_____ The best first aid for a snakebite is to suck the venom, or poison, from the wound.

_____ Snake venom is a kind of saliva.

▶ **Read**

NOTEZONE

Make a note about something you would like to have explained further after reading this.

Allan Bieber is a chemistry professor at Arizona State University. He studies how the toxins, or poisons, in snake venom affect the body's chemical reactions.

SSSSnake Bite

Most toxins in snake venom are proteins.... "Proteins carry out a lot of important functions in cells," says Bieber.

The proteins in snake venom [cause chemical reactions to take place] in the human body, just like our own proteins. For instance, many venoms contain enzymes that set off chemical reactions. But while your body's own enzymes work to help you, the enzymes in snake venom have harmful effects.

Bieber studies the venom of the Mojave rattlesnake.... The Mojave's venom contains a poison called a neurotoxin. Neurotoxins are among the most dangerous kinds of proteins in snake venom. They affect nerve cells, or neurons, and can cause paralysis and eventually, death. Neurotoxins [work by] prevent[ing] neurons from communicating with each other....

Neurotoxins are just one kind of poison found in snake venom. Different snakes carry different kinds of toxins. Some venoms, called myotoxins, damage muscle cells. Others interfere with the blood clotting process. Still others [cause] clotting.

---

proteins: large molecules that carry out chemical reactions in cells

enzymes: proteins that control the rate of chemical reactions in the body

paralysis: being unable to move

clotting: blood cells clumping together into a plug that stops blood flow

From: Boudreau, Diane. "The Virtues of Venom." (http://chainreaction.asu.edu/desert/digin/venom.htm)

FIND OUT MORE

SCIENCESAURUS
Cell Processes	079
Human Biology	083
Chemical Reactions	269

SCiLINKS
THE WORLD'S A CLICK AWAY

www.scilinks.org
Keyword: Chemical Reactions
Code: GSPD23

WHY POISON? All snakes swallow their prey whole. To do that, the prey animal can't be moving. Some snakes coil their body around their prey and squeeze until it suffocates. Other snakes puncture the skin of the prey with their fangs and inject venom into the animal. Once the venom does its job, the snake can actually swallow the whole animal.

   Snake venom is saliva. That's right, snake spit! The table below lists some of the proteins that may be found in snake venom, their effect on a mouse or other prey animal, and their effect on a human.

Protein	Effect on Prey	Effect on Human
Neurotoxin	paralyzes prey; prey dies because breathing stops	stops nerve cells from communicating with each other and with muscles; makes breathing difficult; can cause death due to paralyzed diaphragm (breathing muscle)
Hemotoxin	destroys blood cells; prey dies because of damage to circulatory system	damages blood cells; can cause bleeding at bite wound, internal organs or brain, leading to death
Digestive enzymes	begins to break down body tissues to help the snake digest the prey	tissue damage in the area around the bite

NEUROTOXINS The human nervous system allows for communication between different parts of the body. All your senses depend on nerve cells being able to send information to the brain. Every movement of your body depends on the brain or spinal cord being able to send messages to muscles.

   In the table above, you learned that neurotoxins, which interfere with nerve cell communication, can make it hard to breathe.

▶ *What do you suppose might happen if a snake spit venom with a neurotoxin directly into a person's eye?*

_____

▶ *What other ways can you think of that neurotoxins might affect the victim of a snakebite?*

_____

_____

_____

_____

SNAKES AND PEOPLE When a poisonous snake bites a mouse, it dies. When the same snake bites a human, the human usually doesn't die. Humans have one important factor in their favor—size.

▶ *How might size help a person survive a snakebite?*

_____

_____

_____

Although snake venom is scary stuff, it might have uses in medicine. Tiny amounts of snake venom might be used to help a patient with a disease that causes tremors. Tremors are shaking muscles, and are caused by nerve cells telling muscles to contract too frequently.

▶ *Look back at the table on page 194. What protein in snake venom might be useful for such a patient? Why?*

_____

_____

_____

THINK ABOUT IT There are more species of nonpoisonous snakes than poisonous snakes. But it's important to take any snakebite seriously. Even a nonpoisonous snake's bite can cause an infection.

▶ *How do you think a nonpoisonous snakebite could infect you?*

_____

_____

If someone is bitten by a snake, the person should be taken to a hospital as quickly as possible. It's always good first aid to wash the wound, but don't put ice on it. Don't try to suck out the venom, as you may have seen done in movies. In many cases, this won't remove enough venom to be helpful. And it adds another risk—germs from your mouth may cause an infection.

▶ *Can you think of another safety reason not to try this?*

_____

_____

_____

Now go back to the quiz you took in *Before You Read* on page 192. How did you do? Make corrections as needed.

Reactions in Action

Mind Your Mummy

How can you slow down a chemical reaction? Ask your mummy!

About 5,000 years ago, the ancient Egyptians figured out how to preserve bodies. When a living thing dies, a chemical reaction takes place: Bacteria invade and the body begins to decay. Bacteria need moisture to survive. Egyptians mummified a body by removing the moisture from it. This slowed down the chemical reactions of decay.

NOTEZONE

(Circle) the stages of mummification that you think slowed down decay of the body.

> **Read**

Herodotus, a Greek historian, visited Egypt in 450 B.C. and learned how mummies were made. Here's what he wrote:

HOW MUMMIES ARE MADE

"As much of the brain as possible is extracted through the nostrils with an iron hook, and what the hook cannot reach is dissolved with drugs. Next the [body] is slit open with a sharp ...stone and the entire contents of the abdomen are removed.

"The cavity is then thoroughly cleansed and washed out, first with palm wine and again with a solution of pounded spices. Then it is filled with [herbs] .... The opening is sewn up and then the body is placed in natron for 70 days...."

extracted: removed
abdomen: the part of the body between the bottom of the rib cage and the pelvis
cavity: hollowed-out space

solution: mixture of particles dissolved in a liquid
natron: a salt that absorbs moisture

From: Herodotus. *The Histories*. Penguin Group UK.

SCILINKS
THE WORLD'S A CLICK AWAY
www.scilinks.org
Keyword: Chemical Reactions
Code: GSPD23

UNIT 5: INTERACTIONS OF MATTER

Activity

MAKE A POTATO MUMMY

The ancient Egyptians preserved bodies by mummifying them. See what happens when you preserve a potato.

What You Need:

- one small potato, peeled and cut in two
- salt
- baking soda
- measuring cup
- two disposable plastic cups
- safety goggles

What to Do:

1. Put on your safety goggles.
2. Put one potato piece in each plastic cup.
3. Fill the measuring cup with baking soda up to the $\frac{1}{3}$ mark. Then add salt until the cup is filled to the $\frac{2}{3}$ mark.
4. Mix the salt and baking soda together and pour it into one of the cups. Make sure the potato piece is completely covered with the salt mixture.
5. Put both cups in a dark place for a week.
6. After a week, carefully pour out the salt mixture and take a look. Compare the potato piece that was in the salt to the one that wasn't.

WHAT DO YOU SEE?

▶ *Compare the potato pieces. Describe what you see.*

_____

_____

Propose Explanations

WHAT DO YOU THINK?

▶ *Why didn't the salt-covered potato decay like the other one?*

_____

_____

▶ *Look at the phrases you circled in the reading. How is what you did to the covered potato similar to what the Egyptians did to bodies?*

_____

_____

Energy from Chemicals

Making the Sea Shine

What glows eerily in the dark of night, but isn't a ghost?

Charles Darwin (1809–1892) is best known for his theory explaining the process of evolution. His life in science began at the age of 22. That was when he signed on for a long voyage aboard a ship called the *Beagle*. Darwin was the ship's unpaid naturalist.

The voyage was supposed to last two years but instead lasted five. The trip took Darwin down the Atlantic coast of South America and up the Pacific coast, then through the South Pacific to Australia. Finally, the ship circled around the rest of the world and back to England. In all of these remote places, Darwin had opportunities to observe rocks, plants, and animals that few people had ever studied. Careful observations and brilliant logic helped the young student become an accomplished scientist.

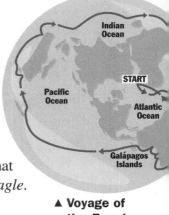

▲ **Voyage of the *Beagle***

NOTEZONE

Circle the words that describe the light Darwin saw.

FIND OUT MORE

SCIENCESAURUS

Relationships
Between
Populations   132
Chemical
Reactions   269
Forms of Energy   300
Light   308

SCILINKS
THE WORLD'S A CLICK AWAY

www.scilinks.org
Keyword: Chemical
Energy
Code: GSPD24

▶ Read

Here is a section from the journal Darwin kept during the *Beagle*'s voyage. It is from December, 1833. The ship was in the Atlantic Ocean, near the Plata River in South America.

Light in the Night Sea

While sailing a little south of the Plata on one very dark night, the sea presented a wonderful and most beautiful spectacle. There was a fresh breeze, and every part of the surface, which during the day is seen as foam, now glowed with a pale light. The vessel drove before her bows two billows of liquid phosphorus, and in her wake she was followed by a milky train. As far as the eye reached, the crest of every wave was bright, and the sky above the horizon, from the reflected glare of these livid flames, was not so utterly obscure as over the vault of the heavens.

spectacle: an unusual sight
vessel: ship
bow: the front of a ship
billow: wave

phosphorus: substance that glows in the dark
wake: the trail left in the water by a moving boat
crest: upper edge

horizon: imaginary line where the sky meets earth or sea
livid: grayish-blue or pale white
obscure: dark
vault: arched roof

From: Darwin, Charles. *The Voyage of the Beagle*. Doubleday & Co.

▶ Explore

MAKE INFERENCES The light Darwin saw came from tiny one-celled organisms called *dinoflagellates* (dy-noh-FLA-juh-letz) swimming near the surface of the ocean water. The light they give off is an example of bioluminescence—light produced by a chemical reaction inside a living organism. Scientists think animals use bioluminescence in various ways. They might use the light to hide from a predator, to blind a predator, or to attract prey.

Dinoflagellates can make light inside their cells by mixing special chemicals. One chemical that is used to make light is called *luciferin*. The cells also have another chemical called *luciferase*. Luciferase is a catalyst. That means it helps the other materials interact, but it doesn't change and is still there at the end of the reaction. When luciferin is mixed with oxygen (O_2), luciferase helps start the reaction that gives off light.

$$\text{luciferin} + O_2 \xrightarrow{\text{[luciferase]}} \text{oxyluciferin} + \text{LIGHT}$$

Most of the time, dinoflagellates keep the luciferin packaged up, separate from the oxygen. But when the dinoflagellates are disturbed, they release luciferin and the light-producing reaction begins.

▶ *Where in the water did Darwin see dinoflagellates glowing? Name all the different places mentioned in the reading.*

_____

_____

▶ *How can you explain why those places were glowing while other places in the ocean water were dark?*

_____

_____

_____

Darwin knew a lot about plants and animals. But he did not know that the light he saw on the ocean's surface was coming from tiny organisms in the water.

▶ *What do you suppose prevented Darwin from knowing that the one-celled dinoflagellates existed? (Hint: Think about what Darwin would need to see the organisms.)*

_____

_____

Energy from Chemicals

Lighting Up the Night

What makes a light stick glow?

Have you ever played with a light stick? You bend or snap the plastic tube and immediately it begins to glow. It might be green or red or purple or yellow. You can wear it around your neck or arm, or put it inside a jack-o-lantern, or just wave it around. You may have also seen light sticks decorating bowling alleys or skating rinks. They're great for outdoor use, too, because they have no electrical parts to keep dry. But, since light sticks don't have batteries or even on–off switches, you may have wondered what makes them work. Where does their energy come from?

▲ Light sticks

Before You Read

YOU'RE GETTING COLDER People get light from many different sources. One thing that many (but not all) light sources have in common is that they produce heat as well as light.

▶ *List five things that give off light.*

_____

_____

_____

▶ *Now put your list in order, starting with the one that gives off the most heat and ending with the one that gives off the least heat.*

_____

_____

_____

UNIT 5: INTERACTIONS OF MATTER

▶ Read

A series of chemical reactions makes light sticks glow.

How Light Sticks Work

Since their invention 25 years ago, light sticks have become a Halloween staple. They're perfect as safety lights for little trick-or-treaters because they're portable, cheap and they emit a ghostly glow. Light sticks...also...make an ideal lamp for SCUBA divers and campers.

...[L]ight sticks use energy from a chemical reaction to emit light. This chemical reaction is set off by mixing multiple chemical compounds.... The reaction between the different compounds in a light stick causes a substantial release of energy....

The light stick itself is just a housing for the two solutions involved in the reaction—essentially, it is portable chemistry experiment.... Before you activate the light stick, the two solutions are kept in separate chambers. [A chemical solution and a dye fill] most of the plastic stick itself. [Another solution], called the activator, is contained in a small, fragile glass vial in the middle of the stick.

When you bend the plastic stick, the glass vial snaps open, and the two solutions flow together. The chemicals immediately react to one another, and the atoms begin emitting light. The particular dye used in the chemical solution gives the light a distinctive color.

---

staple: a regular part of something
emit: give off
substantial: large
housing: a container that holds something

essentially: basically
activate: make active
chambers: spaces
vial: container
distinctive: special

From: Harris, Tom. "How Light Sticks Work." *HowStuff Works.*
(www.howstuffworks.com/light-stick.htm)

NOTEZONE

Underline the important ingredients of a light stick.

Circle the sequence of actions that lead to atoms giving off light.

FIND OUT MORE

SCIENCESAURUS

Compounds	262
Chemical Reactions	269
Forms of Energy	300
Light	308
Electromagnetic Spectrum	309

SCI LINKS
THE WORLD'S A CLICK AWAY

www.scilinks.org
Keyword: Chemical Energy
Code: GSPD24

STEP BY STEP This diagram shows the parts of a light stick.

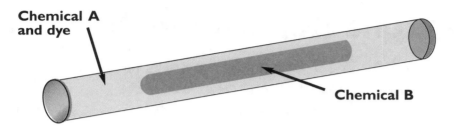

Chemical A
and dye

Chemical B

A chemical reaction causes the stick to glow. The reaction starts when you break the glass vial and ends when the light stick no longer glows. The chemical reactions that produce the light occur in four separate steps.

1. Chemical A reacts with Chemical B to form Chemical C and Chemical D.
2. Chemical C does not react with any of the other chemicals. Chemical D breaks down to form Chemical E and more of Chemical C.
3. Chemical E breaks down to form carbon dioxide (CO_2). When it does, it gives off energy.
4. The dye does not react with any of the other chemicals, but it glows when it absorbs energy.

► *Use this information to make a graphic organizer that shows the chemical reactions that produce colored light in a light stick.*

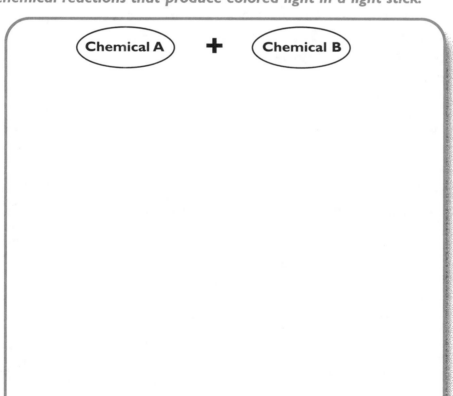

Chemical A ➕ Chemical B

FIND EXAMPLES Light comes from lots of different sources. The light from common, everyday light bulbs is produced when a wire inside the bulb gets so hot that it glows. Light given off by hot objects is called incandescent light. All other light is called luminescent light.

   The table below shows several different kinds of luminescent light. You will probably recognize the type of luminescent light that is often used in classrooms. You learned about another type of luminescent light in lesson 55. Complete the table by adding examples of each type of light. Do research to find examples of types of light you don't know about.

Type of Light		Description	Examples
Incandescent			
light given off by very hot objects		often given off when an object is heated by electricity	
Luminescent			
light given off by objects that have not been heated	**Chemiluminescence**	given off by some chemical reactions	
	Bioluminescence	given off by a chemical reaction inside a living organism	
	Fluorescence	given off by some objects when they are hit by ultraviolet waves	
	Phosphorescence	given off by some objects when they are hit by ultraviolet waves even after ultraviolet waves stop	

Energy from Chemicals

Keeping Toes Warm

When you wish you could take your campfire with you, try this instead.

Throughout human history, people have had to find ways to stay warm in cold places. Of course, some places are colder than others. Dr. Jose Torres teaches classes at the University of South Florida. He also does research that sometimes takes him to unusually cold places.

Dr. Torres studies ecosystems in Antarctica. His work involves being outdoors in extremely low temperatures and extremely high winds. As you can imagine, he wears several layers of clothes designed to trap his body heat. But body heat isn't enough. Fortunately, explorers like Dr. Torres can wear miniature heaters in their clothes.

▲ **Suiting up for a dive**

Before You Read

YOU'RE GETTING WARMER Few people actually travel to the poles and experience arctic weather, but most of us have been unpleasantly cold at one time or another. Your body needs to stay close to 37°C. When the surrounding air is much colder than that, your body's heat energy is rapidly lost to the cold air. To survive extreme cold, you need to be able to trap your body heat and keep the cold away from your skin.

► *Name some cold places you've been and how you stayed warm there.*

_____

_____

_____

_____

_____

46

> **Read**

Here, Dr. Torres describes some of the preparations he goes through before diving under the ice in Antarctica.

Trying Not to Freeze

Our last cruise to the Antarctic took place from the 20th of July to the 1st of September, which is in the middle of the Antarctic winter. We routinely experienced temperatures between −25° and −30°C (−13° and −22°F)....

With this report I will give you a little more detail about what it is like to dive underneath Antarctic ice. Let me begin with the type of gear that we use. First, to protect us from the cold, we use a dry suit. A dry suit is basically a heavy rubber suit that has feet integrated into it, much like an old fashioned pair of long johns. It is sealed at the neck and cuffs with tight latex seals to prevent water from entering....

Under the suit we wear expedition-weight long underwear...as our first layer, then a very thick Polartec® fabric suit as our main barrier against the cold. ...On our feet we wear sock liners under a heavy pair of wool or wool/synthetic socks. On top of the socks go a pair of Polartec® booties.... Between the socks and the booties (and this is a trade secret) go a pair of chemical toe warmers that work just great. They are a little bag of what feels like tiny pebbles that heat up when exposed to air. They last for 8 hours or so. I personally think that they are a genius-level invention.

routinely: regularly
integrated: built-in
long johns: long underwear
latex: rubber
expedition-weight: extra heavy
booties: loose-fitting socks

From: Torres, Dr. Jose. "Diving Under Antarctic Ice!" The University of South Florida. (www.marine.usf.edu/bio/physiolab/current_projects/nbp0104-diving-article.html)

FIND OUT MORE

SCIENCESAURUS
Ecosystems 129
Chemical Reactions 269
Thermal Energy 301

SCILINKS®
THE WORLD'S A CLICK AWAY
www.scilinks.org
Keyword: Chemical Energy
Code: GSPD24

Activity

MAKING TOE WARMERS

Can you make a toe warmer like the one Dr. Torres described?

Part 1: Finding the Right Reaction

What You Need:
- 6 small resealable plastic freezer bags
- iron powder
- salt
- antacid tablets
- powdered detergent
- safety goggles
- 6 thermometers
- measuring spoons
- water

What To Do:
1. Label the plastic bags with numbers 1–6. Put on your safety goggles.
2. Put one antacid tablet in bags 1 and 2. Put 2 teaspoons of powdered detergent in bags 3 and 4. Put 2 teaspoons of iron powder in bags 5 and 6.
3. Add $\frac{1}{8}$ teaspoon of salt to one of the antacid-tablet bags (bag 2), one of the detergent bags (bag 4), and one of the iron-powder bags (bag 6). Seal the bags without squeezing the air out, and shake to mix the contents.
4. Place a thermometer in each bag, making sure it reaches into the materials inside. Record the temperatures in the table.
5. Add 1 teaspoon of water to each of the six bags. Seal each bag without squeezing the air out, and shake it to mix the contents. Open a corner of each bag and reinsert the thermometer, making sure it reaches into the material inside.
6. Observe each bag every 5 minutes for 15 minutes. Record the temperatures.

Time (min)	Temperature (°C)					
	Bag 1 antacid tablet water	**Bag 2** antacid tablet salt water	**Bag 3** detergent water	**Bag 4** detergent salt water	**Bag 5** iron powder water	**Bag 6** iron powder salt water
Start						
5						
10						
15						

▶ *Which of the bags, if any, got warmer?*

_____

_____

▶ *What materials would you use to make a chemical toe warmer?*

_____

_____

Part 2: Improving the Product

What You Need:
- 4 small resealable plastic freezer bags
- toe warmer materials from Part 1
- safety goggles
- sugar
- marbles
- vermiculite
- small piece of wood
- water
- 4 thermometers
- measuring spoons

What to Do:
1. Label the plastic bags with numbers 1–4. Put on your safety goggles. Then prepare four of your toe warmers from Part 1, but don't add the water yet.
2. Put 2 tablespoons of sugar in bag 1. Put 6 marbles in bag 2. Put 2 tablespoons of vermiculite in bag 3. Put the piece of wood in bag 4.
3. Seal each bag without squeezing the air out, and shake it to mix.
4. Measure the temperature in each bag as you did in Part 1.
5. Add 1 teaspoon of water to each of the four bags. Seal without squeezing the air out, and shake to mix. Open each bag and reinsert the thermometer, as in Part 1.
6. Observe each bag every 10 minutes for 30 minutes. Record the temperatures in the table.

Time (min)	Temperature (°C)			
	Bag 1 toe warmer materials sugar water	**Bag 2** toe warmer materials marbles water	**Bag 3** toe warmer materials vermiculite water	**Bag 4** toe warmer materials wood water
Start				
10				
20				
30				

▶ *Which of the bags stayed warm the longest?*

_____

_____

▶ *What materials would you use to make an improved chemical toe warmer?*

_____

_____

Materials Science

STRONGER THAN A SPEEDING BULLET

Which comes first, the invention or a use for it?

What do silk, wood, and nylon have in common? They are all polymers. A polymer is a substance whose molecules are made up of many smaller units strung together in long chains. Some polymers, like silk and wood, occur in nature. Others, like nylon, were invented in a laboratory.

Scientists and engineers use their understanding of chemistry to invent new materials. Sometimes they want to develop a material to fill a specific need. Other times they stumble upon a material and then find a use for it. Either way, the result is new materials that are useful to people.

▲ **Stephanie Kwolek in the lab**

 Before You Read

EFFORT OR LUCK? Was there ever a time when you were trying to do something that you found very difficult? Maybe you even wanted to quit. Did you quit? Or did you keep trying and finally succeed? Or, maybe there was a time when you understood something or did something right away because of sheer luck.

▶ *Think about learning to play an instrument, learning a sport, or perhaps looking for a lost object. Describe why the experience was or was not difficult for you, and whether your success was due to hard work or luck.*

_____

_____

_____

_____

_____

_____

_____

▶ Read

NOTEZONE

Underline the physical properties of the polymer Stephanie Kwolek invented.

Stephanie Kwolek spent most of her time in the lab combining, heating, stirring, and spinning different substances to see what she could create.

Something New Under the Sun

Imagine this. It is 1964. You are a chemist working in a research laboratory of a major company. Your boss has asked you to find new synthetic polymers.... One day, you combine some substances and heat up your mixture carefully, just as you do every day. But this day, something strange happens. The mixture is cloudy instead of clear. When you stir it, it doesn't look the way you expect. Something clicks in your head, and you rush to find the person in charge of testing new polymers. He isn't at all sure he wants to test this strange glop, but, after talking to him for a long time, you convince him. You're just sure there is something unusual about the substance in your test tube. You are right.... You have just invented a brand new polymer that weighs very little but is strong and stiff beyond anyone's imagination. A few years later, your discovery is used to make bullet-resistant vests and helmets. Your name and picture are in advertisements and billboards as the woman who saved thousands of lives.

synthetic: man-made
polymer: substance whose molecules are made up of many smaller units strung together in long chains
substances: stuff, materials
bullet-resistant: difficult or impossible for bullets to go through

From: Howell, Caitlyn. "Kevlar, The Wonder Fiber." Smithsonian Institution. (www.si.edu/lemelson/centerpieces/ilives/lecture05.html)

FIND OUT MORE

SCIENCE SAURUS

Properties of Matter   251

SCI LINKS
THE WORLD'S A CLICK AWAY

www.scilinks.org
Keyword: Physical Properties of Matter
Code: GSPD25

Kevlar products ▶

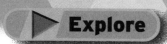

Explore

FIND THE USE The polymer Stephanie Kwolek discovered was later named Kevlar. Inside the box are a number of products that are made from Kevlar. Below the box is a chart that lists some of the properties of Kevlar.

Think about which properties are important for each product. Write the products in the table next to the appropriate properties. (You may write a product in more than one box.)

Products Made from Kevlar	
• airplane body parts	• protective gloves
• automobile brake pads	• rope
• bicycle helmets	• skis
• bullet-resistant clothing	• tennis rackets
• kayaks	

Property of Kevlar	Products
Lightweight	
Will stretch without breaking	
Resists bending	
Does not change size or shape with change in temperature	
Does not cut easily	
Very hard	
Flame-resistant	

THINK ABOUT IT What other use can you imagine for Kevlar in your own life? Think of something you own or use that might work better if it were made of Kevlar. Which properties of Kevlar would be important?

_____

_____

_____

_____

_____

GETTING IT RIGHT Sometimes Stephanie Kwolek experimented with polymers that she or other members of her team had already invented. Other times, she would mix together different substances even though she wasn't entirely sure what the result would be. It was this second, trial-and-error method that produced Kevlar.

▶ *What are the advantages of each method?*

_____

_____

_____

_____

_____

_____

The first light bulb that Thomas Edison invented burned out very quickly. The problem was the filament—the glowing wire inside the bulb. Edison and his team of scientists tested more than 6,000 materials before they found one that made a good filament.

▶ *How was the method used by Edison's team similar to the one used by Kwolek's team?*

_____

_____

Thomas Edison once said, "Genius is one percent inspiration, 99 percent perspiration."

▶ *Look up any words you do not know the meaning of. Then describe what you think Edison meant by this statement.*

_____

_____

▶ *Would you say Kwolek's work was more perspiration or inspiration? Explain your reasoning.*

_____

_____

_____

_____

Materials Science

Lighter, Stronger, Better

Even the most ordinary objects have to come from somewhere.

In the early 1960s, people paid a deposit (a small amount of money) when they bought a bottle of soda pop. They got the deposit back when they returned the bottle. But the bottle was glass, not plastic. "Recycling" meant washing the bottle thoroughly, filling it with more soda pop, and putting it back in the stores.

The plastic soda pop bottle was developed by a man named Nathaniel Wyeth. Nat's father, brother, and sisters were all famous artists. But Nat followed in his uncle's footsteps and became an engineer. He worked for a chemical company called DuPont. DuPont employs engineers and scientists to invent new materials that might be used in new products.

 **Before You Read**

GLASS OR PLASTIC? Think about different drinks and other foods that are sold in glass or plastic jars or bottles. For instance, plastic soda pop bottles are common now, but you can sometimes find glass bottles, too. Apple juice is often sold in plastic bottles but apple sauce is usually sold in glass jars. Which do you prefer? Why? Do you prefer glass for some products and plastic for others? Write some of your thoughts about plastic and glass containers.

_____

_____

_____

_____

_____

_____

_____

UNIT 5: INTERACTIONS OF MATTER

Read

NOTEZONE

<u>Underline</u> the names of the two types of plastic Wyeth worked with.

(Circle) the syllables they have in common.

In order to make a plastic bottle that could hold soda pop, Wyeth first had to improve plastic.

This Would Be Even Better If...

After wondering out loud at work why plastic was not used for carbonated beverage bottles, Wyeth was told that they would explode. He promptly went to a store, bought a plastic bottle of detergent, returned home, replaced the detergent with ginger ale, sealed the bottle, and put it in the refrigerator. The next morning, the bottle had swollen up so much that it was wedged solidly between the refrigerator shelves.

...Wyeth knew that stretching out nylon thread strengthened it by forcing its molecules to align. The challenge he faced was stretching plastic so that its molecules would align in two dimensions, rather than just one. He managed this by creating a "preform" mold...with screw threads running...in a diamond criss-cross pattern. When the plastic was pressed...through this mold, the molecules aligned in the...fashion Wyeth intended. [Then he replaced] the polypropylene material he had been using with polyethylene-terephthalate ("PET"), which has superior elastic properties. The final product was light, clear, resilient, and safe: a complete success.

---

carbonated: made fizzy by the addition of carbon dioxide

wedged: jammed; stuck

align: line up

dimensions: directions

polypropylene: a type of plastic

polyethylene-terephthalate: another kind of plastic

elastic: returns to its original shape

resilient: easily returned to its original shape after stretching or bending

From: Dorchak, Joshua. "Inventor of the Week: Nathaniel Wyeth." *Invention Dimension (MIT).* (web.mit.edu/invent/www/inventorsR-Z/wyeth.html)

FIND OUT MORE

SCIENCESAURUS

Properties of Matter 251
Nonrenewable Material Resources 331
Conservation of Material Resources 336

*SCI*LINKS.
THE WORLD'S A CLICK AWAY

www.scilinks.org
Keyword: Physical Properties of Matter
Code: GSPD25

Explore

ADD A DIMENSION Wyeth improved plastic by changing the way its molecules line up. In old plastics like nylon, the molecules line up in one dimension. In Wyeth's plastic, the molecules line up in two dimensions.

Look at these diagrams of the molecules in two different kinds of plastic.

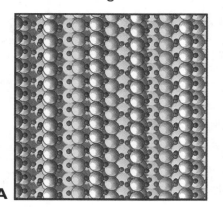

A

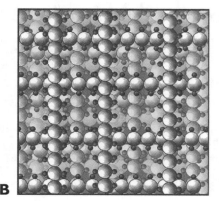

B

▶ *Which diagram shows the molecules aligned in two dimensions?*

_____

When long molecules of plastic are lined up side by side, the plastic is strong in the direction of those molecules.

▶ *On diagram A, draw arrows to show which way the material could be pulled without being stretched out of shape. Explain how you know.*

_____

_____

▶ *On diagram B, draw arrows to show which way the material could be pulled without being stretched out of shape. Explain how you know.*

_____

_____

Early plastic bottles would burst if they were filled with carbonated liquid. Wyeth's plastic bottles do not.

▶ *Using the diagrams, explain why this might be.*

_____

_____

_____

_____

The table compares some of the properties of glass and PET soda pop bottles.

Property	Glass Soda Pop Bottles	PET Soda Pop Bottles
Weight	Heavier to transport to store, and from store to home	Only 6% of the weight of a glass bottle
Clarity	Thick glass made it hard to see the contents	Very thin and clear, easy to see contents
Breakability	Could shatter into sharp pieces when dropped, causing cuts	Shatterproof
Scratch	Scratch when bottles rub up against one another	Not easily scratched by other PET plastic

▶ *Which property might be most important to people who buy one bottle at a time from a vending machine? Explain.*

_____

_____

▶ *Which property do you think is most important to people who buy soda pop at the grocery store? Explain.*

_____

_____

▶ **Take Action**

A CREATIVE FAMILY Nathaniel Wyeth's father, N.C. Wyeth, was a famous painter and illustrator. His brother Andrew was probably the most famous American artist of the 20th century. His sisters Henriette and Caroline were also painters, and Ann was a composer.

Think of the skills and personality traits that would make someone a good inventor. How are they similar to the skills and traits that would make someone a good artist? How are they different? List your ideas in the Venn diagram below.

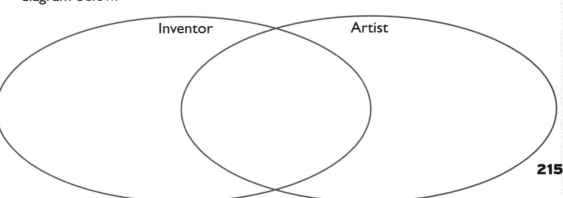

Inventor   Artist

Materials Science

Sticky Business

Why does adhesive tape stick to things?

From the beginning of civilization, people have used adhesives. The ancient Egyptians made paste from flour and water. Other peoples used tree sap or beeswax to stick things together. Most of the products you use today are inventions from the 1900s. That's when scientists began to focus on improving adhesives in the laboratory.

NOTEZONE

Underline the name of the force that makes things stick to themselves.

Circle the name of the force that makes things stick to something else.

FIND OUT MORE

SCIENCESAURUS

Properties of
Matter   251

SCILINKS
THE WORLD'S A CLICK AWAY

www.scilinks.org
Keyword: Physical
Properties of Matter
Code: GSPD25

 **Read**

Benjamin E. Russ from the University of California at San Diego talks about why tape sticks to itself and other things.

I'M STUCK ON YOU

...There are two fundamentally different components of tape's sticky nature; adhesion and cohesion. Adhesion is the binding force between two different materials, whereas cohesion is the binding force between two similar materials. When two materials are brought into contact with each other, the surface molecules interact.... When the molecules are similar, as in the case of two "glue molecules," the cohesive force causes the glue to stick to itself. When the molecules are dissimilar, as in the case of a glue molecule and a molecule of the substrate (the surface the glue is sticking to), the adhesive force holds the glue to the substrate. Hence, the "stickiness" of tape is caused by a combination of the molecular forces of the glue material sticking to itself as well as holding onto the substrate.

fundamentally: basically
components: parts

interact: have an effect on each other
dissimilar: not alike

From: Russ, Benjamin E. "Ask the Experts." *Scientific American.com*
(www.sciam.com/askexpert_question.cfm?articleID=000E47BD-6690-1C71-9EB7809EC588F2D7&catID=3)

Activity

LET'S STICK TOGETHER

There's an adhesive for every need.

What You Need:
- assorted adhesives (clear cellophane tape, masking tape, cloth adhesive tape, self-stick note, etc.)
- sheet of paper, cut into small squares
- small squares of cardboard

What to Do:
1. Test the cohesion of each adhesive. Fold the sticky side back on itself, being sure to leave the two ends unstuck. Press the halves together, then try to pull them apart. Decide whether the cohesion is poor, good, very good, or excellent. Record your observations in the chart below.
2. Test the adhesion of each adhesive. Stick it to the paper, the cardboard, and a desktop. Press it down, then try to pull it off. Record your observations in the chart.

Adhesive	Cohesion	Adhesion
cellophane tape		
masking tape		
cloth adhesive tape		
self-stick note		

WHAT DO YOU SEE?
► *Which adhesive(s) showed the greatest cohesion?*

_____

► *Which adhesive(s) showed the greatest adhesion to the paper? to the cardboard? to the desk?*

_____

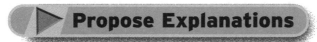

► Propose Explanations

APPLY KNOWLEDGE
► *How do the adhesive properties of self-stick notes make them well-suited to their job?*

_____

Glossary of Scientific Terms

A

acceleration: change in an object's speed or direction (its velocity) over time

acid: any compound that produces hydrogen ions (H^+) in water, and reduces its pH to below 7

adhesion: the force of attraction between molecules of two different substances

alternating current (AC): flow of electricity through a conductor, in which electric charges change direction many times per second

amplitude: total distance a wave moves (oscillates) from its resting position

atmosphere: layers of air surrounding Earth

atom: smallest particle into which an element can be divided and still have the properties of that element

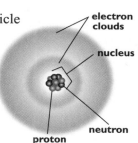

electron clouds

nucleus

neutron

proton

atomic mass: average mass of one atom of an element

atomic number: number of protons in the nucleus of one atom of an element

aurora: display of light in sky, usually at high latitudes; formed where particles from the sun enter Earth's atmosphere and magnetic field

B

bacteria: one-celled organism that lacks a true nucleus; sometimes causes disease

balanced forces: occur when the total of all forces on an object equals zero and the object's motion does not change

base: any compound that produces hydroxide ions (OH^-) in water and raises its pH to above 7

battery: a device that converts chemical energy into electrical energy

binary code: code used by computers that represents all data with strings of 0s and 1s

boiling point: temperature at which a substance changes from a liquid state to a gaseous (vapor) state

bond: a force of attraction that holds atoms, ions, or molecules together; also called **chemical bond**

C

catalyst: substance that helps start or speed up a reaction between two other substances, without being changed by the reaction

cell: basic unit of structure and function in living things

charge: *See electric charge*

chemical: any element or compound

chemical bond: *See bond*

chemical change: occurs when one or more substances are changed into new substances with different properties; cannot be undone by physical means

chemical reaction: change that takes place when two or more substances (reactants) interact to form new substances (products)

chemistry: the study of the structure, properties, and interactions of matter

circuit: path that electric current flows through; a closed circuit has no breaks; an open circuit has a break and current cannot flow through it

cohesion: the force of attraction between molecules of the same substance

colloid: a mixture containing tiny particles of one substance scattered evenly throughout another

color: light of various wavelengths; the eyes see each wavelength of light as a different color

compound: matter made of two or more elements; the elements in a compound are chemically bonded and cannot be separated by physical means; a compound has properties that are different from the elements that make it up

compound machine: a machine made of two or more simple machines that work together

concave: curved in

conductor: substance that conducts heat readily; also a substance that allows an electric current to pass through it

convex: curved out

crystal: a solid made up of molecules arranged in a regular, repeating pattern

current: *See electric current*

D

data: collected information, the results of an experiment or other investigation

direct current (DC): flow of electricity through a conductor, in which electric charges move in only one direction

E

electric charge: a property of the particles in an atom; may be positive (protons), negative (electrons), or neutral (neutrons)

electric current: the amount of electric charge that moves past a certain point each second; measured in amperes (A)

electrical energy: form of energy that consists of the flow of electric charges through a conductor

electricity: general term for interaction of electric charges

electromagnet: magnet made by passing an electric current through a wire wrapped around an iron rod

electromagnetic spectrum: full range of electromagnetic waves

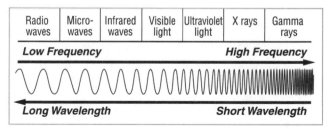

Electromagnetic Spectrum

electromagnetic wave: form of energy that can travel through empty space as well as through matter; includes visible light, radio waves, X rays, and many other wavelengths

electron: negatively charged particle found outside the nucleus of an atom

electron cloud: in the electron cloud model of the atom, region around the nucleus where an electron may be found

electronics: relating to devices that work by controlling the movement of electrons

Glossary of Scientific Terms

elements: substances that are the building blocks of all matter; an element is made up of one kind of atom

energy: ability to do work

energy levels: in an atom, specific areas at definite distances around the nucleus; each energy level can hold a specific number of electrons

engineer: a person who uses knowledge of science to design machines, systems, or products

environment: surroundings and conditions in which an organism lives

enzyme: a protein in the body that helps control a chemical reaction, such as digestion

experiment: series of steps that, under controlled conditions, produces data that test a hypothesis or prediction

exponent: the number above and to the right of a base number that tells how many times to multiply the base number by itself

F

focus: to adjust lenses so that an image is clear and sharp

force: a push or a pull

freezing point: temperature at which a substance changes from a liquid state to a solid state; same as **melting point** for that substance

frequency: the number of wave vibrations (oscillations) produced in one second; measured in hertz (Hz)

friction: force that resists the motion of two surfaces that are touching each other

G

gamma ray: a type of high-frequency electromagnetic wave

gas: matter that has no definite volume or shape; for example, air

gear: a wheel with teeth, sometimes considered a simple machine

gene: segment of DNA, found on a chromosome, that determines the inheritance of a particular trait

gravitational potential energy: energy stored in an object due to its height above ground

gravity: force of attraction between any two objects

H

habitat: the place in an ecosystem where an organism lives

heat: transfer of thermal energy between substances that are at different temperatures; sometimes used to mean thermal energy

heat energy: total kinetic energy contained in all the particles of a substance; also called thermal energy

hertz (Hz): measurement of wave frequency equal to vibrations per second

humidity: amount of water vapor in the air

hypothesis: an idea that can be tested by experiment or observation

I

incandescent: producing light as a result of being hot

inclined plane: simple machine that consists of a flat, sloping surface (ramp); *See also screw and wedge*

infrared: a type of electromagnetic wave with a frequency just less than the frequency of red light

insulator: a material that does not transfer heat energy easily; also a substance that does not allow electric current to pass through it

ion: atom or molecule that has an overall electric charge due to loss or gain of electrons

K

kinetic energy: the energy an object has because it is moving

L

laboratory: a workroom with equipment for scientific research

lens: curved, transparent piece of glass or plastic that bends light rays to form an image

lever: simple machine made of a long rigid bar that rests on and turns around a support called a fulcrum

light: a type of energy that humans can see; part of the electromagnetic spectrum

liquid: matter that has a definite volume but not a definite shape; for example, water

luminescent: producing light without getting hot

M

magnet: object that attracts iron

magnetic field: region of magnetic force around a magnet

magnetic force: the attractive or repulsive force that acts between magnetic materials; strongest at the poles of magnets

magnetic pole: one of two ends of a magnet, called north and south, that produce opposing forces

mass: amount of matter in something; measured in grams (g)

matter: the material that all objects and substances are made of; anything that has mass and takes up space

mechanical wave: energy that travels through matter; examples include sound, ocean waves, and earthquake waves

melting point: temperature at which a substance changes from a solid state to a liquid state; same as **freezing point** for that substance

metallic bond: bond that holds metal atoms together; positive metal ions are surrounded by a sea of shared electrons

metals: elements, usually solid, with a shiny surface; metals conduct electricity and heat energy well; examples include gold, iron, lead, copper, and silver

mixture: a combination of two or more substances that have not combined chemically and that can be separated by physical means

model: a simplified version of some part of the natural world that helps explain how it functions

molecule: smallest particle of a substance that still has the properties of that substance

motor: a machine that uses electricity to produce movement

N

negative charge: *See electric charge*

neutron: in an atom, particle with a neutral charge; located in the nucleus

Newton's First Law of Motion: An object at rest will stay at rest unless acted on by an unbalanced force. An object in motion will stay in motion at the same speed and in the same direction unless acted on by an unbalanced force.

Newton's Second Law of Motion: The acceleration of an object by a force is inversely proportional to the mass of the object and directly proportional to the force.

Newton's Third Law of Motion: For every action, there is an equal but opposite reaction.

nucleus: the center of an atom, made up of protons and neutrons

O

optics: the study of light and vision

organ: in an organism, structure made of two or more different tissues that has a specialized function; for example, the lungs

organic chemistry: the study of compounds that contain the element carbon

organism: a living thing

P

patent: a government document giving a person the sole right to make, use, and sell their invention for a set period of time

periodic table of elements: a chart where all elements are organized into periods and groups according to their properties

physics: the study of energy, forces, and motion

pitch: how high or low a sound is; determined by the sound's frequency

plastics: chemical compounds that can be easily shaped into many different products; often made from refined petroleum

pole: *See magnetic pole*

pollution: any change in the environment that is harmful to organisms

polymer: a substance whose molecules are made up of many smaller, identical molecules

positive charge: *See electric charge*

potential energy: stored energy an object has because of its position or shape

power: the amount of work done or energy used in a unit of time

prediction: a guess about what will happen under certain conditions, that is based on observation and research

pressure: amount of force exerted on a given area by an object or substance; SI unit is the pascal (Pa)

property: characteristic of a material that helps to identify or classify matter

proteins: organic compounds that make up living things and are essential for life

proton: positively charged particle located in the nucleus of an atom

pulley: simple machine consisting of one or more wheels with a rope wrapped around them

R

reaction: *See chemical reaction*

receiver: a device that converts electro-magnetic or electric signals to sound or light

reflection: bouncing back of a wave from a surface

resistance: measure of how much a material opposes the flow of electric current through it

robot: a machine that can carry out a variety of tasks automatically

S

scientific notation: a way of writing extremely large or extremely small numbers; uses a number between 1–10 multiplied by a power of 10, such as 9.8×10^6

screw: a simple machine consisting of an inclined plane wrapped around a cylinder

simple machine: a device that makes work easier by changing the size or direction of the force applied to it

solar energy: energy from the sun in the form of heat and light

solid: matter that has a definite shape and volume; for example, a rock

solute: *See solution*

solution: mixture in which the molecules of one substance, known as the **solute**, are dissolved in another substance, known as the **solvent**; the solute is present in a smaller quantity than the solvent

solvent: *See solution*

sound: energy that travels through matter as mechanical waves, and can be heard by the ear

specific heat: thermal energy needed to change the temperature of 1 gram of a substance by 1°C

speed: distance traveled by an object in a given amount of time

states of matter: the forms matter can take, as in liquid, solid, or gas; also called phases of matter

static electricity: electricity in which electric charges build up on an object; the movement of the charge off the object is called electric discharge or static discharge

suspension: mixture in which particles of a solid are spread throughout a liquid, and the particles are large enough to settle out

T

technology: the use of scientific knowledge and processes to solve practical problems

temperature: measure of the average kinetic energy of the particles in a substance; measured in degrees Celsius (°C) or degrees Fahrenheit (°F)

theory: an idea that is the best explanation of many observations and helps make new predictions

thermal energy: *See heat energy*

tissue: in plants and animals, a group of cells that work together and do a specific job

transformer: device used to change the voltage of an alternating current

transmitter: a device that sends out signals, usually electrical or radio wave

U

ultrasound: any sound wave whose frequency is too high to be heard by humans

ultraviolet light (UV): a part of the electromagnetic spectrum that is invisible to humans; also called ultraviolet radiation and ultraviolet rays

unbalanced force: occurs when the net force on an object does not equal zero; results in the object changing its motion

V

vacuum: a complete absence of matter

velocity: an object's speed and direction at a given instant

vibration: a rapidly repeated back-and-forth movement over a short distance

voltage: the difference in electrical energy per unit of charge at two different points in a circuit; measured in **volts (V)**

volts: the SI unit of electrical energy per unit of charge

volume: Measurement: amount of space an object or substance takes up; measured in liters (L) or cubic centimeters (cm³); Sound: loudness

W

wave: a back-and-forth motion that travels from one place to another

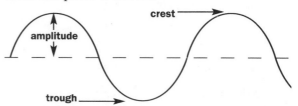

wavelength: distance from any point on one wave to a corresponding point on the next wave, such as crest to crest or compression to compression

wedge: simple machine consisting of an inclined plane that moves

weight: a measure of the force of gravity on an object; directly related to an object's mass

wheel and axle: simple machine made of a shaft (the axle) inserted through the middle of a circle (the wheel)

wind: movement of the air caused by differences in air pressure

work: occurs when a force is used to move an object through a distance; measured in joules (J)

X

X ray: very high frequency electromagnetic radiation; can be used to make images of the human body by passing radiation through the body onto photographic film